SEAWOLVES
Pirates & the Scots

ERIC J. GRAHAM

BIRLINN

This edition first published in 2007 by
Birlinn Limited
West Newington House
10 Newington Road
Edinburgh EH9 1QS

www.birlinn.co.uk

ISBN13: 978 1 84158 580 2
ISBN10: 1 84158 580 7

British Library Cataloguing-in-Publication Data
A catalogue record for this book is available from the British Library

Book design by James Hutcheson
Typeset by Waverley Typesetters, Fakenham
Printed and bound by Cox & Wyman, Reading

Contents

The Earlier Wave of Pirates in the Indian Ocean,
1695–1705

The Last Pirates in Scottish Waters, 1821

Foreword

Pirates! Eric Graham has a riveting tale to tell. Too much of Scottish history is either ill-written text or retold romance. Not this: it is an account of brutal criminals preying on legitimate merchants sometimes scarcely less brutal than themselves, of sensational crimes and short lives (few pirates outlived their thirtieth birthday), and it is a story of law enforcement equally cruel and often grossly unjust. It goes with pace: it is informed by original records form the Scottish Admiralty Court, many unused before. It uncovers a world of historical fact unimagined by most of us.

In Scottish literature, it was Robert Louis Stevenson who was the unrivalled master of pirate stories, but the journalism of Daniel Defoe and the folklore collecting of Walter Scott predated and informed *Treasure Island*. Until now, few historians have explored this topic, and when Eric Graham does so he discovers a truth harsher than fiction, but no less colourful. What novelist could outdo the contemporary description of Bartholomew 'Black Bart' Roberts, pirate captain, fighting to his death dressed in a 'rich crimson damask waistcoat and breeches, a red feather in his hat, a gold chain round his neck, with a diamond cross hanging to it, a sword in his hand and a pair of pistols hanging at the end of a silk sling, hung over his shoulder'? Or imagine crimes more awful than the mutilations, rapes, tortures and casual executions of their prisoners that were the pirates' stock in trade? Or generosity more ostentatious than that of the former pirate hunter and Governor of Madras, Captain James Macrae, who returned from his adventures to make his simple cousins rich and their humble daughter (by dint of a huge dowry) the thirteenth Countess Glencairn?

Underneath the detail and the drama, however, lie some remarkably important discoveries relevant to the history of Scottish trade. The Glasgow merchants became famous for their part in the tobacco trade. But Eric Graham shows how they were equally attracted in the first years after the Union to the slave trade, only to be scared off it by their losses to the pirates who cruised the African coast as well as the Caribbean. The great age of the pirates lasted from the late seventeenth century to the 1720s and was brought to a close by the Royal Navy. How would the Scots have fared without its protection? Not well, to judge by the many disasters that befell ships of the Darien Company when they tried to sail in the Indian Ocean.

This is a book of few heroes, and of many villains of almost unimaginable wickedness, but you did not have to be a pirate to be a blackguard. The story of the captain and crew of the *Worcester*, the English East Indiaman, who were arrested, tried and executed for piracy even as evidence was being presented of their innocence, is a tale of political expediency and moral cowardice that engulfed the highest in the land.

Piracy still exists, of course, in the West Indies and off Indonesia. The last pirates in Scottish waters were a Swede and a Frenchman executed in Edinburgh in 1822 after trying to come ashore in Lewis with their ill-gotten gains. We are certainly well rid of them. This splendid book explains it all.

CHRISTOPHER SMOUT

Acknowledgements

My gratitude goes out to the members of the Early Scottish Maritime Exchange (ESME) whose unstinting help so enriched this work. I am particularly obliged in this instance to Tom Barclay, David Dobson, Michael Dun and Sue Mowat.

Sue requires a special mention as her meticulous cataloguing of the records of the High Court of Admiralty of Scotland – undertaken without pay and little official recognition – has done so much to open up this neglected field in Scottish history.

My heartfelt thanks go to my wife, Jan, who has willingly forgone six months of my regular earnings to make this happen and given of her precious days' leave to read and comment on this book. For this, and everything else, I love her dearly.

Finally, I must thank Birlinn Limited for their faith in the concept.

Introduction

Hollywood has largely moulded the general perception of pirates. This image is highly romanticised and often light-hearted, and the setting is, invariably, the Caribbean. In this account, following in the tradition of Daniel Defoe and Robert Louis Stevenson, the wanton savagery of piracy and the injustices of the system that both nurtured and persecuted those who chose to join the 'Brethren of the Coast' are left unsanitised.

The principal story-line follows their trail of destruction and mayhem out from the Caribbean, along the coasts of the Americas, Africa and into the Indian Ocean. In its course, the growing network of Scots abroad and their early involvement in the slave and Far Eastern trades are revealed.

With the exception of the last chapter, this book examines the Scots engagement with the 'Golden Age of Pirates' (1690s–1720s) which, like the Wild West in American history, lasted only a few decades. Events revolved around a handful of highly dramatic characters, most of whom originated from the pirate nest of New Providence in the Bahamas and so knew each other. Their wicked lives and audacious exploits mesmerised the hedonistic society of Hogarth's London and shocked the good burghers of Edinburgh. It also spawned a new industry – the journalism of crime.

The timing of the first great outbreak of global piracy was not accidental. The eviction of Catholic James and the installation of Protestant William and Mary on the English and Scottish thrones – the Glorious Revolution of 1688 – sparked the Second Hundred Years War with France and her bullion-rich ally Spain. With their government's blessing, hundreds of vessels took out a privateering commission with the Admiralty to capture, as legal prize, the shipping of the enemies of King William and (after 1702) Queen Anne. The richest prizes sought were the Spanish bullion galleons returning from the New World and East Indiamen carrying the luxuries of the Far East.

Chasing French East Indiamen took them round the Cape of Good Hope into the Indian Ocean and the Red Sea. There they encountered the Great Mogul's fleets carrying bejewelled pilgrims to and from Mocha (the landing port for Mecca). Given such a temptation, it was, as Captain Kidd found to his cost, but a small step to lose irreversibly the protective status of a legal privateer and acquire that of a hunted pirate.

During the short periods of peace, many ships' companies chose not to return to the harsh world of serving for a pittance on a merchantman or navy vessel. They chose instead to continue to raid wherever and whomsoever they pleased. Their actions quickly threatened the fragile European treaties and agreements made with foreign potentates. To appease their critics the government was forced on a number of occasions to take drastic action to destroy their nests.

This succeeded in scattering them further afield. Unfortunately for the Scots, this coincided with their first great push to break into the world markets. It follows that Scots featured in every aspect of the piracy story from serving as a 'Blade' (fighting man) onboard a pirate ship, to the captains pursuing the pirates (including several of the colonial Governors sponsoring the chase). The Scots were, therefore, highly instrumental in shaping the course of pirate history.

Piracy trials heard before the High Courts of Admiralty sitting in Edinburgh and London provide the core source of this book and offer an array of insights into this brutal (and at times astounding) world of rogue mariners sailing in the times of Robinson Crusoe.

The order in which they are examined follows closely that of their appearance in the early editions of Captain Charles Johnson's *General History of Pyrates* – the incomparable contemporary source on the Golden Age of Piracy. The first edition (1724) related, in great detail, the life and times of the New Providence pirates (1715–25). The later 1726 edition added the tale of Orcadian pirate John Gow along with short biographies (real and imaginary) on the earlier wave of Indian Ocean pirates (1695–1705). This chronological back-tracking also mirrors my own 'voyage of discovery' which started as a young student at the foot of Captain Macrae's mausoleum in my native Ayrshire.

Concluding this study with the last piracy trial heard in Scotland was simply irresistible. Had the updating of Johnson's *Pyrates* continued after 1730, I am sure that Heaman and Gautier would have joined the pantheon of pirates in the 1822 edition.

It is intended that, by starting with the New Providence Pirates, the reader will readily acquire an understanding of the origins, ways and lifestyle of the Black Flag pirates. This is not so forthcoming with the short accounts of the earlier Indian Ocean pirates who did so much damage to Scottish trading aspirations in the East.

Most pirates started out as members of a single company sailing under an elected captain. Their first vessel was usually a small sloop, cut to take more cannon and swivels (a type of small cannon) and manned by around thirty Blades. If they were successful in taking a larger vessel, they invariably transferred their accumulated armaments to her, thereby dramatically increasing their chance of taking a plate galleon or an East Indiaman.

This 'trading up' in vessels and firepower occasionally led to the creation of a pirate flotilla, manned by hundreds of Blades and commanded by the 'aristocrats' of piracy – who referred to themselves as the members of the 'House of Lords'. Such a force was more than a match for a solitary East Indiaman or a rag-tag garrison of a remote slaving fort. The destruction and carnage they were capable of inflicting was immense and had the directors of the various Royal Companies and the marine insurers of London clamouring at the doors of the Board of Trade and the Admiralty for naval counter-measures.

Given the anarchic nature of pirate associations, these deadly flotillas had a short lifespan, as their captains invariably quarrelled, usually after a drunken carousal, and then sailed away taking their company with them. Not even the most feared and ruthless captain, such as Bartholomew 'Black Bart' Roberts, could hold a flotilla of them together for more than a few months at a time.

A pirate captain faced the eternal quest for a treasure-laden prize, one that would provide his men with the means to bribe their way into a retirement of luxury ashore. Few achieved this goal. For many, the daily struggle was to find smaller prey to loot for provisions to feed their large extravagant crew and the marine stores to maintain their vessel.

A pirate captain's control over his crew was tenuous at the best of times. Only during the heat of battle was the captain's authority unchallenged. On all other occasions, the pirates' notion of a floating democracy gave the grumbling factions below decks the right to challenge him on a whim. This situation led the more determined captains to draw up Articles of Regulation with which to curb the excesses of his men – particularly with gambling, drink and women.

Their rate of squandering of provisions, goods, vessels and life was staggering high. Disease and drunken violence ensured that few pirates lived beyond the age of 30. To maintain their numbers and fighting capability, all captains resorted to taking men off captured vessels – particularly skilled sailors. These 'forced' men were made to work the ship under threat of death and often alongside enslaved Africans. Many succumbed to the reign of terror and turned pirate by signing the Articles.

It is one of the quirks of pirate history that most sought to emulate the great pirate, Captain Avery, and retire back to Britain. Once there, they could vanish into the sprawling metropolis of London as rich men. To minimise the risk of being identified and hanged, it was necessary to make a landing from a small vessel on deserted beach in a remote part of Britain. After scuttling the vessel, the company would then split up into small groups and walk to the nearby towns. There, with a little prudent spending, they could transform themselves into gentlemen before heading for London.

The west coast of Scotland provided the conduit for the retiring rump of 'Black Bart' Roberts's crew, the most determined and vicious group in pirate history. A number of them, however, found themselves in Edinburgh Castle dungeons, having given themselves away by their drunken and riotous behaviour on the road from Inveraray to Greenock.

Their trial in Edinburgh (1720) provides the student of the Golden Age of Piracy with a unique insight into the New Providence captains and their crews. It also fills in previously missing details of Davis and Roberts's extensive cruises off the Caribbean, African and Brazilian coasts. These were by far the most devastating and bloodiest of the era. One of their casualties was Scotland's aspiration to join in the slave trade.

Of the other two Black Flag piracy trials heard before this court that against Captain Green and the crew of the *Worcester* (1705) has the greatest significance to the course of Anglo-Scottish relations. Indeed, the execution of Green and two of his officers on Leith Sands – to the jeers of a mob of 80,000 – triggered the Act of Union of 1707.

The myriad of documents generated by these piracy trials and disputes over slaving voyages are matched with the personal letters and printed broadsheets and newspapers which abound in the archives and libraries of Scotland and beyond. In collating these sources one crosses the path of the greatest writers on pirates: Daniel Defoe, Robert Louis Stevenson and Walter Scott. These literary connections are explored throughout the course of the narrative.

In this second edition the chapter on Robert Louis Stevenson & the Pirates has been revised to include extracts from his letters that relate to his use of Johnson's *Pyrates* and other authors on pirates.

Glossary of Seventeenth- and Eighteenth-century Maritime Terms

Types of vessel

Brig or brigantine – A two-masted, square-rigged, wide-decked sea-going vessel of various sizes. The 'Aphrodite' brig has a mixture of two rigs: square sails on the main and schooner rig on the mizzen (rearmost) mast.

Cutter – A single-masted vessel, fore and aft rigged, with 'sharp' hull and extended bowsprit flying one or two jibs.

East Indiaman – Any vessel hired or owned by the East India Company. The largest were those employed exclusively by the Company, known as a 'regular berth'. These were well armed and carried large crews for their defence. They were often seconded by the government to support the navy in times of war.

Galleon – A old term that was used to describe a large vessel with a characteristic very high stern and low bow. This design was first developed by the Portuguese and Spanish as ocean-going ships. The names later became synonymous with treasure (plate) ships.

Galley – A sailing vessel pierced for sweeps (large oars) that could propel the vessel in light airs. These required large numbers of crewmen. This use of the term dies out by the mid-eighteenth century. In the Mediterranean, it also describes the very low freeboard vessels primarily driven by banks of oars manned by slaves or convicts.

Lugger – A small two-masted vessel with lug square sails that can be set to work high to windward. Much favoured by smugglers and inshore privateers.

Schooner – A 'fore-and-aft' rigged vessel, commonly deployed in American and West Indian waters.

Ship – A three-masted, all square sail, decked vessel.

Sloop – The general term for small single-decked vessels, usually singled-masted and without cutter bow or extended bowsprit.

Snow – A variation of the brig rig where the mizzen mast has a separate upright pole attached, from which the trysail is set without a lower boom yard.

Yacht – A decked hull with superior passenger accommodation, originally of Dutch design, which was dedicated to the conveyance of an important person or persons.

Yawl – A small two-masted vessel where the mizzen mast is stepped behind the tiller.

Sailing terms

Careening – Beaching a lightened vessel at high tide after which she is hauled over on one side for cleaning. A particularly important piece of maintenance in tropical waters, where the boring worm quickly destroys a hull if not burned off.

Flotta – The annual convoy of Spanish and Portuguese treasure ships crossing the Atlantic from the 'New' to the 'Old' World.

Forecastle (pronounced fo'c'sle) – The forward superstructure of a vessel where most of the ordinary crew have their bunks.

Jury-rigged – Temporary repairs made to a vessel after losing a mast or masts that allowed her to get under way again. This usually involved lashing spars to what was left of the mast so that a sail could be hoisted.

Kedging – Hauling a grounded vessel off by her own anchor. This involved rowing the anchor lashed to her long-boat out to deeper water. After it was dropped, the crew on board the vessel would haul her up by the cable, using the capstan.

Letter of Marque – A legal document granted to a master to act as a privateer in times of war. This allowed him the right to seize the merchant vessels of a specified enemy by force. These impressive documents were issued by the Admiralty after the master had given bond as to his good conduct during the cruise.

Prize – A vessel condemned in the Prize Court of the Admiralty as legally taken in times of war by a naval commander or a master of a commissioned privateer.

Privateer – A private vessel commissioned by a 'Letter of Marque' to take the merchant vessels of a named enemy state in wartime. When at war with more than one state, the master was required to carry a number of 'letters', each covering a specified nationality of combatant.

Purser – A person appointed by the owners of the vessel to oversee the financial aspects of her maintenance and seamen's wages and victuals. He was also responsible for collecting passenger fees and allocating berths.

Supercargo – A person appointed by the owners of a cargo to trade on their behalf. He normally had experience in stocktaking and bookkeeping. While he had no say in the daily handling of the vessel, he usually decided which ports would be visited in a trading venture. In extended voyages he normally took a 'second supercargo' (usually a trainee) and clerk with him.

Tacking – Working a sailing vessel upwind by a series of zig-zag manoeuvres.

Tons – At this time, a vessel's size was always referred to by her 'tons burthen' (carrying capacity in the hold). There was no concept of displacement tonnage until the nineteenth century.

General terms & money

Bombo – A drink made with lime juice and raw sugar cane boiled together, into which a spirit was usually added.

Cutlass – A heavy curved cleaving blade with hand-guard, much favoured by pirates and ordinary seamen.

Guinea – A large English (British after 1707) gold coin named after the African source of gold dust.

Hanger – A short sword favoured by gentlemen.

Moidore – A large Portuguese gold coin.

Pagoda – A large Indian gold coin minted at Madras.

Pieces of eight – A large Spanish silver coin worth eight 'reals' produced in vast numbers at their South American mints.

Plate – A generic term for gold and silver bullion in all its forms, coins and bars.

Punch – A mixture of spirits (usually rum) and raw sugar cane boiled up and served in a bowl.

Swivel cannon – A small cannon that was mounted along the deck rail of a vessel which usually fired a pound weight of grapeshot.

Trade goods – Those items made specifically to meet the requirements of a local native market. Trade guns were particularly crude in their manufacture.

Select Who's Who
of Pirate Captains

Henry 'Long Ben' Avery (or Every, alias Bridgeman)

English-born. Turned pirate for the second time off Corunna (May 1694). Cruised with Thomas Tew. Disbanded his crew at New Providence, Bahamas (June 1696). Retired to Devon.

Pirate Vessel: *Fancy* (ex-privateer *King Charles II*) – seized off Corunna (May 1694), wrecked at New Providence, Bahamas (June 1696).

Stede Bonnet

Resident of Barbados. Turned pirate 1717. Cruised with Edward 'Blackbeard' Teach. Hanged at Charleston (November 1718).

Pirate Vessel: *Revenge* (later renamed *Royal James*) – legally owned by Bonnet, captured by Captain Rhett in Cape Fear River (Autumn 1718).

John Bowen

Welsh-born founder of pirate settlement of Maritan, Madagascar. Retired to Mauritius (1702).

Pirate Vessels: *Speaker* (ex-slaver of that name) – wrecked off Mauritius (1701).

Speedy Return (ex-Company of Scotland merchantman) – seized at Maritan, Madagascar (July 1701), burned at Rajapore, India (August 1702).

Content (ex-Company of Scotland merchantman) – seized at Maritan, Madagascar (July 1701), burned at St Augustine, Madagascar some months later.

Defiance (ex-Moorish prize) – seized off Malabar Coast (August 1702), given to Captain Howard when crew disbanded at Mauritius some months later.

Howell Davis

Welsh-born resident of New Providence, Bahamas. Turned pirate after taking the pardon (Autumn 1718), killed in an ambush on the island of Principe, West Africa (July 1719).

Pirate Vessels: *Buck* – seized in Privateers Bay, Hispaniola (Autumn 1718) and abandoned off Fort St James, Gambia River, West Africa (February 1719).

King James (ex-Liverpool merchantman) – seized off Isle de Mayo, Cape Verde Islands (1719), abandoned off Fort St George, Anamaboe, West Africa (June 1719).

Royal Rover (ex-Ostender *Mark De Campo*) – seized off Cape Three Points, West Africa (May 1719) and burned to the waterline off Bermuda by Kennedy (December 1719).

Edward England

Resident of New Providence, Bahamas. Turned pirate after taking the pardon (1718), died Madagascar (1720/21). Cruised with La Bouche and Taylor. Was marooned on Mauritus by Taylor.

Pirate Vessels: *Royal James* (ex-merchantman *Pearl*) – probably seized off Guinea Coast.

Victory I (ex-merchantman *Peterborough*) – seized off Guinea Coast (1719), burned at Madagascar (1723).

Victory II (ex-East Indiaman *Cassandra*) – seized at Isle de Johanna, Comoro Islands (August 1720) and later surrendered to Spanish at Porto Bello (1723).

John Gow (alias Smith)

Scottish-born resident of Stromness. Turned pirate off the Canaries (November 1724); hanged at Wapping (June 1725).

Pirate Vessel: *Revenge* (ex-merchantmen *Caroline*, later renamed *George*) – seized off the Canaries (November 1724), captured by naval party in Calf Island, Orkney (February 1725).

Walter Kennedy

Irish-born resident of New Providence, Bahamas. Turned pirate with Howell Davis off Hispaniola (Autumn 1718), hanged at Execution Dock, London (July 1721). Served under Davis and Roberts.

Pirate Vessels: *Buck* – seized in Privateers Bay, Hispaniola (Autumn 1718) and abandoned off Fort St James, Gambia River, West Africa (February 1719).

King James (ex-Liverpool merchantman) – seized off Isle de Mayo, Cape Verde Islands (late 1718 or early 1719), abandoned off Fort St George, Anamaboe, West Africa (June 1719).

Royal Rover (ex-Ostender *Mark De Campo*) – seized off Cape Three Points, West Africa (May 1719) and burned to the waterline off Bermuda (December 1719).

Flying Eagle (ex-*Eagle* of New York) – seized off Jamaica (December 1719), abandoned in Craignish Loch, Scotland (February 1720).

William Kidd

Scottish-born resident of New York. Commissioned privateer and pirate hunter. Hanged for murder and piracy at Wapping (May 1701).

Pirate Vessels: *Adventure* galley – launched Deptford 1695, sank at St Mary's Isle, Madagascar (April 1698).

Quedah Merchant – seized off Surat (January 1698), abandoned at Hispaniola (May 1699).

Antonio – purchased at Hispaniola (May 1699), arrested at New York (June 1699).

Olivier 'La Bouche' Levasseur

French-born, resident of New Providence, Bahamas. Turned pirate after taking the pardon (1718). Cruised with Davis, Cocklyn, England and Taylor. Hanged at Réunion (July 1730).

Pirate Vessels: *Indian Queen* (ex-merchantman) – seized off Guinea Coast (1719), wrecked at Mayotte, Comoros Islands (July 1720).
Victory I – seized off Guinea Coast (Summer 1719), burned at Madagascar (c. 1723).

Bartholomew 'Black Bart' Roberts

Welsh-born third mate on the slaver *Princess*. Forced by Davis at Anamaboe, West Africa (June 1719), soon turned pirate, killed off Cape Lopez in action against HMS *Swallow*, Captain Ogle (February 1722). Served under Davis, replaced him as captain after his death.

Pirate Vessels: *Royal Rover* (ex-Ostender *Mark De Campo*) – seized off Cape Three Points, West Africa (May 1719) and burned to the waterline off Jamaica (December 1719).

Royal Fortune I (ex-Bristol merchantman) – seized off Newfoundland (1719).

Royal Fortune II (ex-French merchantman) – seized off Newfoundland (1719).

Royal Fortune III (ex-Royal Africa Company *Onslow*) – seized off Liberia (August 1721), captured by HMS *Swallow* off Cape Lopez (February 1722).

John Taylor

Resident of New Providence, Bahamas. Turned pirate (1718) with Edward England. Served as quartermaster until he replaced England as captain (1720). Took a Spanish pardon at Porto Bello and entered the service of the Costa Guarda (1721).

Pirate Vessels: *Royal James* (ex-merchantman *Pearl*) – probably seized off Guinea Coast (Spring 1719).

Victory I (ex-merchantman *Peterborough*) – seized off Guinea Coast (Summer 1719), burned at Madagascar (c. 1723).

Fancy (ex-Dutch merchantman) – abandoned at Isle de Johanna, Comoros Islands (August 1720).

Victory II (ex-East Indiaman *Cassandra*) – seized at Isle de Johanna (August 1720) and later surrendered to Spanish at Porto Bello (1723).

Edward 'Blackbeard' Teach (or Thatch or Drummond)

Resident of New Providence, Bahamas. Turned pirate 1717. Cruised with Stede Bonnet. Killed in fight with Lieutenant Maynard in Ocracoke Inlet (November 1718).

Pirate Vessel: *Queen Anne's Revenge* – captured in Ocracoke Inlet, North Carolina (November 1718).

The New Providence Pirates, 1715–25

CHAPTER 1

Captain Macrae
& the Pirates

L ate in 1731 a life of relentless grinding poverty was miraculously alleviated for an Ayrshire carpenter and his large family. At the doorstep of their cottage was a messenger with a gift of 100 pounds, a small fortune by the measure of the day. The overawed householders, Hugh and Bella Maguire, were informed that their benefactor was a retired 'nabob' of great wealth who would visit them soon.

Overjoyed and filled with great expectations, they celebrated. The elder children were sent out to buy a sugar loaf and a bottle of brandy from the local smugglers. The sugar loaf was carefully scooped out and the cavity filled with brandy; whereupon the whole intoxicating concoction was, with the help of large spoons, heartily devoured by all.

Their mysterious benefactor was Bella's long-lost cousin, James Macrae, one-time East Indiaman captain, pirate hunter, Governor of Madras and now resident of Blackheath, Kent. Isabella had last seen him as a boy, shortly before he absconded aboard a ship clearing out of his homeport of Ayr. He had run away from a life of near starvation, leaving behind his widowed mother, who could barely feed him on her meagre earnings as a washerwoman. As he was her only child, his departure left her to face certain destitution in her old age, had not the Maguires taken her in and cared for her to her dying day. Forty years on, the prodigal son had returned intent on redeeming his name and repaying their kindness and humanity.

As an exceedingly rich man with no immediate family of his own, Macrae's generosity knew no bounds. The Maguire family were soon installed in their new home, the fine farm of Drumlow, Ochiltree, while their five gifted young children received an education and 'finishing' at a boarding school, as befitted their new social status.

A decade later, Macrae returned to Ayrshire to preside over their adult future, acquiring his own estate of Orangefield in the nearby coastal village of Monkton. His first concern was to secure an advantageous marriage for their eldest daughter, Elizabeth, who had been working as a farm servant. His choice of suitor was William Cunningham, the impoverished thirteenth Earl of Glencairn. This haughty nobleman set aside his deeply held social scruples to the proposed union when he was informed that her dowry was £45,000 in diamonds, and the Barony of Ochiltree – an estate worth a further £25,000.

Thereafter, Elizabeth, as Countess Glencairn, overcame her husband's thinly disguised scorn at being married to a 'violer's daughter' (her father Hugh was a well-known sixpenny fiddler at local weddings) to become a greatly respected member of Scottish society. She never forgot her lowly upbringing and set up a school in the area to teach local girls spinning. She and her son, the fourteenth Earl, were much-loved patrons of the local poet Robert Burns and highly influential during his sojourn in Edinburgh.

Macrae successfully repeated this social metamorphosis with the Maguires' two sons and other two daughters. The eldest son, James, was settled with the great Houston estate in Dumfriesshire, which included the surrounding parish, on the condition that he assumed the surname 'Macrae'. His younger brother, Hugh, inherited the Drumdow estate from his parents. The middle sister, Margaret, was married to the advocate Charles Erskine of Barjarg (later Lord Justice Clerk), who used her dowry to buy the great Alva estate. Macrae's favourite, the youngest daughter, christened Macrae Maguire in his honour, was left the residue of his £100,000 fortune and his Orangefield estate, on his death in July 1746.

Macrae died a man redeemed from his actions as a youth, reconciled to his family and honoured by his own people. With his approval, Glencairn loaned £1,500 of Elizabeth's dowry towards the £5,000 ransom demanded by Bonnie Prince Charlie's invading Jacobite army to forgo the sacking of Glasgow. Prior to their arrival, Macrae had openly demonstrated his allegiance to the Hanoverian Succession by presenting that town with a grand equestrian statue of his hero, William of Orange. This was erected at Glasgow Cross at a cost of £3,000. Its swivel-mounted metal tail has been a great favourite for generations of children and Hogmanay revellers alike. It can still be seen near Glasgow Cathedral.

How this Ayrshire-born son of a washerwoman came by his immense wealth is the very stuff of adventure stories. One part of his dynamic career – that in the service of the Honourable East India Company – was the centrepiece of *Annuals*, compiled in 1863 by J. Talboys Wheeler, Professor of Moral Philosophy and Logic at the Madras Presidency College. Closer to home, his fairytale patronage of the Maguires captivated local commentators during his lifetime.

It was left, however, to Daniel Defoe, the great historian of Black Flag pirates (writing under the *nom de plume* Captain Charles Johnson in 1724) to immortalise Macrae as both the defiant victim and the persecutor of some of the most celebrated villains of the time.

Captain Macrae won his place in Defoe's *A General History of the Robberies and Murders of the Most Notorious Pyrates* by virtue of his heroic deeds on the blood-strewn deck of the 380-ton East Indiaman *Cassandra* in the Indian Ocean on 17 August 1720.

The *Cassandra*, on hire to the East India Company, had rounded the Cape of Good Hope with a 'regular berth' company ship, the *Greenwich*, under Captain Richard Kirby and in company with a Dutch Ostend Company ship. They had set aside trade rivalries to sail together as mutual defence against the pirate squadrons that were then heavily infesting African and Indian waters. Their destination was the Isle de Johanna in the Comoros Islands in the northern throat of the Mozambique Channel which separates Africa from the giant island of Madagascar. Once there, they intended to water, before heading out into the relative safety of the Indian Ocean.

At daybreak on 27 July, they approached this emerald jewel of a natural anchorage with trepidation, as it was a haven frequently used by pirates to careen their fouled hulls. To do this they had to unship their cannon, beach their vessel and haul her over on her side to burn off the barnacles and boring worms. As this was the most vulnerable time for a pirate crew, they usually sought a remote island. On this day there was no pirate vessel to be seen in the bay, but on shore they espied a party of fourteen heavily armed Europeans.

From the local islanders, who canoed out to greet them, they found out that these armed men were a hunting party that had detached themselves from the pirate crew of the *Indian Queen*. This was the flagship of the French pirate Olivier Levasseur of Calais, known to all as 'La Bouche' (a corruption of the French word for 'Buzzard'). He had captured this Dutch East Indiaman (250 ton and 28 guns) off the Guinea Coast but, following a botched attempt to careen her, she now lay wrecked on a reef off the nearby island of Mayotte. The party on Johanna were hunting for fresh provisions while amusing themselves by trying to make contact with the pirates from the great Captain Avery's crew, who were rumoured to have gone native on this island.

La Bouche, with the remaining forty crew of the *Indian Queen*, was still on Mayotte, thirty-five miles away. There they were labouring to salvage her guns, main timbers, iron fixtures and rigging to equip a new vessel they were attempting to build from local wood.

Macrae had followed in La Bouche's wake and witnessed the wanton destruction that he and his kind had wrought on the shipping and slaving stations along the 3,000 miles of the Guinea Coast over the past two years. He did not, therefore, hesitate to call a Council of War on the *Cassandra*. At that meeting Kirby and his Dutch counterpart swore to support him steadfastly in his plan to sail immediately to Mayotte and eradicate this nest of murderers while the pirates were relatively helpless.

Around midday, they got under way from the sheltered anchorage at Johanna. As the leading *Greenwich* and the 'Ostender' emerged from under the lee of this volcanic island's lofty peaks to the crack of canvas filling with the oceanic trade winds, there appeared two sails bearing down from the open sea. They were the pirate flotilla led by the infamous Edward England, returning to their island lair after looting a Moorish prize they had carried off to St Mary's Isle, Madagascar. This barbaric affair involved torturing the passengers for their hidden possessions before butchering all of them.

Macrae on the *Cassandra*, being last to weigh anchor, was caught making slow headway towards the open sea in the fickle light airs of the bay. As the two pirate ships swooped in to block his escape, England let fly his personal black flag with skull and crossbones from the mainmast of his ship, the *Victory* (46 guns). Macrae, with a clear view from his quarterdeck, was left in no doubt as to his fate should he offer resistance, as a blood-red flag – the sign that no quarter would be given if he chose to fight – flew from the pirate's foremast.

So trapped, Macrae swung the *Cassandra* round to engage them and win the time needed for his consorts to come to his assistance. Under Macrae's resolute command, his well-manned East Indiaman of thirty cannon had every prospect of holding them at bay. Indeed, his first broadside smashed into the *Victory*, holing her between 'wind and water', forcing England to sheer off on the opposite tack to make emergency repairs and to tend his wounded. The smaller *Fancy* (40 guns) under the command of England's hot-tempered and brutal lieutenant, John Taylor (alias Jaspar Seagar), now took the lead.

With the die now cast for a bloody fight, Macrae frantically fired his signal cannon for the *Greenwich* to come to his rescue. Kirby, by now a good league out to sea, ignored all such pleas and chose instead to hove-to with the Ostender to watch the ensuing battle. As Macrae bitterly reported to his superiors later, *he basely deserted us and left us engaged with barbarous and inhuman enemies with their Black and Bloody red flags hanging over us and no appearance of escaping being cut to pieces.*

Abandoned and committed, Macrae brought the *Cassandra* round to present her broadside to the closing *Fancy*, exhorting his officers and men to continue to ply their cannon for their very lives. It was a desperate gamble, as the pirates' vastly superior numbers would seal their fate should they get alongside. This tactic succeeded in keeping the *Fancy* at bay for over three hours. By around four o'clock in the afternoon, as the casualties mounted on the pirate brig from the relentless bombardment, the infuriated Taylor ordered his crew to man their sweeps and row the *Fancy* up to the *Cassandra* for boarding and the kill. Macrae countered by having his gunners rake her water line, smashing the giant oars to pieces.

England, having completed his running repairs to the *Victory*, returned to the affray, forcing Macrae to play his last card. This was to run the *Cassandra* close inshore till she grounded, side-on to his pursuers. As the *Fancy* had a much shallower draft, Taylor saw his chance finally to get alongside the stationary East Indiaman. As fate would have it, the *Fancy* hit a sand bar and came to a shuddering halt, half a pistol-shot length from the *Cassandra*. Stuck with her bow facing the East Indiaman, the pirates could not bring their main cannon to bear. Macrae's men seized on their opportunity to pour a series of devastating broadsides into the grounded brig. At such close range, the carnage amongst the pirate gunners was so terrible that they were soon forced to abandon the main deck cannons and take cover under hatches.

It was, however, to be a pyrrhic victory for Macrae. He later claimed that, had Kirby joined him, they would easily have taken both pirate vessels. As it was, England on the *Victory* had now closed sufficiently for his cannons to sweep the *Cassandra*'s quarterdeck, killing a number of Macrae's officers. Under this murderous covering fire, England dispatched three boatloads of fresh men over to the *Fancy* to kedge her off and man her abandoned guns. By five o'clock Kirby, standing on the deck of the *Greenwich* safely out at sea, had seen enough and sailed away – as Macrae put it, *leaving us struggling in the very jaws of Hell.*

Two hours later, as the first grappling iron from the *Victory* swung over the stern of the *Cassandra*, Macrae gave the order for all hands to abandon ship. Under cover of the swirling acrid smoke from his cannons and incoming grenades, most of his crew – some in the long boats, others swimming – made for the shore.

In the dash for safety, Macrae was forced to leave behind ten dead and three severely wounded crewmen. The latter were cut to pieces within minutes of the first wave of enraged boarders hitting the deck. Out of the combined pirate companies of 500 men, close to 100 of their comrades had been killed by Macrae's defiant salvoes. This had been the longest and bloodiest engagement of their reign of terror along the African coast. Indeed, this was the most costly encounter with a merchantman in pirate history. It can be taken as certain that, had they laid hands on Macrae and his crew, they would have been massacred out of hand.

As it was, the pirates swarming over the deck of the *Cassandra* could do little more than shoot wildly into the jungle where their prey had vanished with the fading light. In the ensuing hiatus, their leader, Edward England, skilfully deflected the blame for the whole blood-soaked fiasco with a £2,000 reward for Macrae – dead or alive.

At first light the following day Macrae, despite a musket-ball wound to his head, led his bedraggled and exhausted men on a day-long forced march. Their destination was the main native village some twenty-five miles inland from the scene of the sea battle. He must have visited this place and made allies on a previous voyage, for this was the court of the African 'King' of the island who gave them not only food and shelter, but his royal protection from the pursuing pirates. As his men recovered in a concealed place, Macrae had his native hosts put it out that he had died of his wounds during the trek through the jungle. On hearing this story, his pirate pursuers gave up their manhunt and returned to the *Cassandra* to claim their share of the spoils.

Ten days later, the remarkable Macrae retraced his footsteps and audaciously presented himself to the pirates on board the *Cassandra*. He was counting on the passage of time and their pleasure at finding on board the East India Company's annual investment of £75,000 to curb their bloodlust long enough for him to negotiate a ransom for his ship and what he could of its valuable cargo of trade goods.

Macrae's astonishing display of bravery, returning alone and unarmed, greatly impressed Edward England and many of his crew. But not so with the more ruthless John Taylor, who spoke for the aggrieved faction that was for cutting him down where he stood. As Daniel Defoe recounted, at the critical moment in this contest of wills, *a Fellow with a terrible pair of whiskers, and a wooden Leg, being stuck round with Pistols, like the Man in the Almanack with Darts, came swearing & vapouring upon the quarterdeck.* Placing himself between Macrae and his would-be executioners, he shook the Scottish captain's hand, heartily bellowing, *Shew me the man that offers to hurt Captain Macrae and I'll stand to him, for an honester fellow I never sailed with!*

There were others amongst the assembled Brethren who also knew and respected him, sufficient to end the dispute and save his life. Such widespread recognition strongly suggests that, as a younger man, Macrae had once sailed the Caribbean with this kind of company. This theory gains further support from the fact that, not only was he spared, but later a mellow drunken Taylor whimsically agreed to let him have the badly shot-through *Fancy* and some of the bulk cargo out of the *Cassandra*. This munificence was later to prove a grave error of judgement for many of the 'Blades of Fortune' then assembled on the deck of the *Cassandra*.

Macrae's sense of survival dictated that he should extract himself while Taylor was still intoxicated. Once ashore he kept out of sight during the days the pirates took to convert his old command to serve as a pirate ship. On completion, England transferred his flag to the *Cassandra* while Taylor moved up to command his patched-up and leaky old *Victory*.

On the morning of 3 September, as they pulled up their anchors to get under way, Macrae made one more appearance. His mission was to plead for the release of his second mate, John Lazenby, whom they had managed to lay hands on and 'forced' to join their company as their pilot for their intended cruise of the Malabar Coast of India. Macrae was unsuccessful with this request.

On their departure Macrae immediately summoned his crew from their hiding places and set them to work on the *Fancy*. Using materials abandoned by the pirates, they got her hull into a barely seaworthy condition to resume their voyage to Bombay, under a jury-rig and flying discarded old canvas.

Macrae's powers of command and seamanship were, once again, put to the test. Becalmed for much of the time out in the expanse of the Indian Ocean, they endured a passage of forty-eight days. During that time in the searing heat, he strictly rationed his destitute and half-crazed crew to a pint of water a day per man.

On his arrival at Bombay (16 November) he lodged his report of the loss of the *Cassandra* with the governor. It was at odds with that submitted earlier by Kirby who claimed he had tacked the *Greenwich* back into the bay to aid Macrae, only to find the *Cassandra* already aground. Kirby also stated that he had been chased back out to sea by a pirate vessel that almost got within cannon range of the *Greenwich*. To escape its clutches he had to cut adrift the long boat and a yawl he was towing and crowd on all sail. During the chase he lost his main topmast along with two seamen.

There was no official inquiry as to the discrepancies between the two accounts. The damage, however, was done and Kirby's reputation lay in tatters. He was later reported to have died of shame the following August whilst ashore at Bandar Abbas.

Macrae's tenacity and martial talent were not lost on the Honourable Masters of Bombay, then the principal 'factory' of the East India Company on the west coast. The timing of his arrival was fortuitous as they were in desperate need of such a man. Only days before, their fleet of locally-built oared galleys led by four fully-armed East Indiamen – *London, Britannia, Defiance* and *Revenge* (towing the massive floating gun battery *Phrahm*) – had suffered a humiliating retreat from before the fortress of Gheriah. This was the stronghold of the great Indian warlord and pirate king, Congalee Angria. His domain stretched some

250 miles along the Malabar Coast and was protected by some forty forts.

Their retreat had turned to a rout on their way back to Bombay when, during the night, they ran into England, Taylor and La Bouche. Macrae's old adversaries had crossed the Indian Ocean in the *Cassandra* and the *Victory* in search of richer prey. Whilst they had no intention of linking up with Angria, the company's admiral, an incompetent clerical administrator by the name of Brown, assumed otherwise and ordered his fleet to stand away.

This submissive manoeuvre emboldened England who, though out-gunned and outnumbered, seized the opportunity to run his two ships down their line, pouring broadsides into the *London*. Her commander, the timorous Captain Upton, refused to fire a shot in reply or engage without Brown's express approval and *security for all such damage as the ship might sustain*.

This farce turned into a general panic when Brown, instead of issuing battle orders, decided to scatter his fleet to minimise losses to capture. To expedite his escape he cast off the giant gun-battery barge after it was set ablaze. His actions enraged the vast majority of the officers and men and caused an immediate collapse of morale throughout the fleet.

It was a disaster that exposed the company's naval weakness and ineptitude to rival European companies, native enemies and would-be allies alike. To retrieve this dire situation, the highly competent Governor Boone of Bombay ordered Brown back to sea immediately, but with Macrae in effective command. Brown's face-saving order was to confront and defeat these pirates at all costs. Macrae's first act was to unleash the fighting spirit of his commanders by relegating Brown to the role of bystander.

At the first sight of his quarry, Macrae had his fleet cleared for action and bore down under a full press of canvas to engage. England and his pirates had recently found out who was now hunting them from the very drunken John Fawkes, master of a small trading vessel they had boarded. Knowing full well what Macrae was capable of, they ran for it in *a tempest of passion*. During the ensuing three-hour chase, the pirates exploited their superior numbers and seamanship to work their sails to full advantage and so made good their escape.

Expelled from Indian waters, they skulked back towards Mauritius. Lazenby, the forced pilot, later gave evidence to the East India Company directors that the pirates spent much of their time discussing what tortures they would inflict on Macrae, should they fall in with him again. It was during this heated debate that Taylor seized the moment: *the villain that we treated so civilly as to give him a ship and other presents, and now to come armed against us? He ought to be hanged, and since we cannot shew our resentment on him let us hang the dogs who wish him well if clear, Damn England!* With the support of other malcontents this challenge was put to the vote. The result of this pirate-style democracy was that England was deposed and, with three others (no doubt the one-legged pirate included), marooned on the wildest coast of Mauritius.

Once rid of their discredited leader, Taylor transferred his flag to the *Cassandra*, which he renamed the *Victory*, while La Bouche was elected captain of his old charge. Under their new leaders, the pirates' luck changed, and in a most spectacular way. They fell in with the dismasted and badly storm-damaged Portuguese galleon, *Nostra Senhro de Cabo*, in the harbour of Isle Bourbon (La Réunion). It was eight in the morning of 8 April when they attacked her from both sides. They met with little resistance as most of her seventy guns had been jettisoned in the typhoon.

She was the richest prize ever taken in pirate history. Apart from the 200 slaves on board, she was laden with a fortune in diamonds (valued at £500,000) and precious objects (£375,000) belonging to the retiring Viceroy of Goa, the Conde de Ericeira. When added to the booty they already had from the *Cassandra* and their other prizes, the grand total of their haul was in excess of one million pounds.

Lazenby was finally released at Isle Bourbon, by which time he reckoned that there were some 240 pirates left from the two companies that took the *Cassandra*. Each of these pirates' share was a staggering 5,000 guineas in gold and 42 diamonds. He also remarked that one pirate, not content with his lot, used his pistol butt to shatter one very large stone he was given, so that he could boast that he had more diamonds than his shipmates.

By then the game was all but up. Under tremendous political pressure from the Mogul Court and the desperate pleas of the East India Company, the British government finally responded. Commodore Thomas Matthews was dispatched with a naval squadron of four warships with orders to eradicate the pirate nests.

At St Augustine's Bay on the western shore of Madagascar, Matthews left a letter stating his orders and intentions for the commanders of his cruisers who had been scattered by a storm when rounding the Cape of Good Hope. When Taylor and La Bouche arrived at St Augustine, the natives unwittingly handed this letter over to them, as they were European captains.

So forewarned, Taylor had the good sense to quit the pirate business whilst ahead and cleared out of the Indian Ocean on the new *Victory* (ex-*Cassandra*) in December 1722. His last act of piracy was to bombard a Dutch fort on the West African coast before he crossed the Atlantic.

Back in Caribbean waters, Taylor tried to negotiate a pardon with the Governor of Jamaica, the Duke of Rutland, but was refused. Thereafter, he used his immense booty to procure a pardon from the Spanish Governor of Porto Bello on the Isthmus of Darien. To secure the deal, he also offered his vessel and services to the notorious Guarda Costa to hunt interloping dyewood loggers along the Bay of Campechy.

La Bouche stayed on in the Indian Ocean and managed to evade his pursuers, reportedly burying most of his treasure on one of the Seychelles islands. He then tried to emulate his old sailing partner, Christopher Condent, and buy a pardon from the French Governor of Isle Bourbon, after burning the very leaky 'old' *Victory* at Madagascar. It was not long, however, before he was back to his old ways and was eventually captured after a fierce battle with a French frigate. He was hanged for piracy at Isle Bourbon in July 1730. He left behind a cryptic note as to the location of his treasure hoard that has yet to be deciphered.

The marooned England and his fellow companions managed to build a small boat and sail around the coast of Mauritius to the main port. From there they eventually made it back to St Mary's Isle, Madagascar, where they lived on the charity of their fellow pirates. England died soon afterwards at New Mathelege (Masselege) whilst being entertained by an old shipmate and 'King of Madagascar', James Plantain.

'Lord' Plantain was born at Chocolate Hole, Jamaica, and had served his time with the Brethren at New Providence. He was on the *Fancy* with Taylor when the *Cassandra* was taken, and retired soon afterwards to settle in Madagascar with *a harem, a Scotsman and a Dane*. The fate of the one-legged saviour of Macrae remains a mystery to this day.

Macrae, having saved the Company's tenuous hold on Malabar Coast from an onslaught of pirates, was rewarded with a special commission as a 'Superintendent' of the Company. He was also given the task of sorting out their wayward settlement on the west coast of Sumatra. This mission allowed him to pursue his dual interests of weeding out rank corruption and chasing pirates.

Such was his effectiveness in these primary tasks that he was appointed to the presidency of Fort St David (south of Madras) on his return. This position in the 'land service' placed him directly in line to succeed to the presidency of Madras, the second most important British factory in India after Bombay. He did not have to wait for long, as this office became vacant in January 1725. For the next five years he set about restoring the company's credibility with the native rulers and traders, and hence its profitability.

In doing so, however, he made many enemies who insidiously worked, in both Bombay and London, to tarnish his name and reputation. By late 1730 he had had enough, and resigned his highly lucrative commission to retire to Scotland.

His skirmishes with pirates, however, were not over. On his homeward voyage his ship was taken, off the coast of West Africa. In the general confusion, Macrae managed to hide his personal cache of diamonds before stepping forward to negotiate a very small ransom on behalf of the company for such a valuable ship and cargo.

How Macrae amassed his incredible cache of diamonds has never been explained. In his letters home from India in September 1727 to his fellow Scot and mentor, John Drummond of Quarrell, he claimed he was impoverished. This predicament he blamed squarely on the onerous duties of the two years he had already spent as governor of the presidency of Madras (with a £500 annual salary): *as for my remitting money home ... I don't expect great matters if I stay here this seven years, the work I have to do, and what remains incumbent on me, make it impracticable to gett much money.*

The reality would seem somewhat different, as he also enquired after the diamond, *the finest little stone I have ever seen here*, that he had sent as a present to Drummond. This was, no doubt, a placatory gesture as Drummond was a director of the Honourable East India Company and had recently reprimanded him for taking diamonds as presents from the local merchants.

What is clear from his letters is that he had already collected a circle of fellow Scots around him, a number of whom he dispatched on independent trading missions to China. In reporting these highly lucrative ventures, he portrayed himself to their mentor as a long-suffering patriarch, only looking out for their best interests.

A case in question was that of the *imprudence of Mr Campbell* whose solo attempt at diamond dealing had left him grossly overdrawn on his credit, on which Drummond stood guarantor. Macrae blamed much of Campbell's monetary problems on the latter's very young *vain, empty Flirt of a wife*. Macrae's solution was to pack Campbell off on the East Indiaman *Shawburn*, with

2,000 pagodas (gold coins) on yet another six-month trading venture to China. Campbell went as second supercargo under *my brother* Captain John Hunter and watched over by the purser Mr Wedderburn. Campbell left very reluctantly and in bad humour. In his absence, Macrae, *out of pure friendship*, made it his duty to visit the young wife to counsel her on her waywardness.

These selfless social duties aside, Macrae was an ardent reformer. In his first year in office as President of Madras, he greatly reduced expenditure and thoroughly revised slack practices at the mint. He also introduced a new and more realistic exchange rate between gold and silver. He saw it as his civic duty to set up the first Protestant mission in Madras in 1726. The following year he had the city and its suburbs surveyed, in advance of tackling the public sanitation problem that was the cause of the soaring death rate.

As the champion of good business, he set about curbing the wanton excesses of his short-sighted predecessors. Rather than swindle and abuse the local native merchants, he introduced radical reforms that ensured fair dealing and legal recourse. Such popular measures, no doubt, explain their gifts of diamonds to him.

In his self-appointed role as the company's anti-corruption crusader, he made it his business to confront the notorious sharp practices of his senior, Mr Walsh, the recently appointed Governor of Bombay. To do this, he personally sailed the thousand miles round southern India from Madras to Bombay. He arrived just as Walsh was about to sail for Britain. In a matter of days Macrae exposed to the governing council the elaborate web of false book-keeping that Walsh had devised to cover his extortion and fraudulent activities.

Having once again saved the Company from a humiliating scandal, Macrae received their gratitude while the disgraced Walsh was sent home without his ill-gotten fortune. His replacement, Robert Cowan, was a Scot from Macrae's circle.

Back in London, the much-aggrieved Walsh worked relentlessly to turn the tables on Macrae, accusing him of gross misconduct and misappropriation. Macrae had anticipated such mischief and tried to defend himself with Drummond by denouncing Walsh first, *who no doubt will bespatter me for the hardship done him ... I assure you he is a composition of falsehood and Jesuitical hipocrisy and I re[al]ly take him to be as Very a knave as ever serv'd: disserv'd: the Company, for he's one that will stick at nothing to gett money.*

Despite this pre-emptive strike, Walsh's allegations, when added to those of others, had the desired effect and the Court of Directors ordered an investigation into Macrae's activities. At the centre of their inquiry was the behaviour of his chief Dubash – Gooda Anconda – over whom he was meant to have firm control. This native ruler was notorious for corruption and oppression among his own people.

Although Macrae survived their inquiries with his reputation largely intact, it undermined his commitment to his appointment. In February 1730 he wrote to Drummond announcing his intention to resign: *Your last letter hath quite tired me of this station & hope to get leave to quit it with the next shipping. I could with patience bear all the little Artifices made use of to make me leave the Government till this last shock wherein the Malice & Lies invented by my Enemies and industriously improv'd by a friend of yours, hath impos'd so far on the Court of Directors, as to make them write so many biting reflections against me.*

Unlike Walsh, Macrae left behind no personal records of his financial dealings for his successor to scrutinise. Since the death of the company-appointed secretary, *poor Pyat*, in May 1727, from *drinking punch to great excess*, followed by a bout of consuming *Madeira & water to most Exorbitant degree*, Macrae had taken upon himself the onerous task of keeping his own accounts.

He resigned from the presidency in December 1730 and sailed from Madras (21 January 1731) with a fortune estimated at £100,000 sterling (the equivalent today of in excess of £10 million), of which £45,000 was in pouches of diamonds on his person as he boarded. It would seem that his services to the company came at a high price.

Scotland's national poet, Robert Burns, was an indirect beneficiary of the Macrae legacy. The latter's great financial investment in the social promotion of his two favourite Maguire sisters, the eldest Elizabeth and the youngest Macrae, came to timely fruition just as the bard contemplated his move from his native Ayrshire.

Macrae Maguire's husband, the impetuous James Dalrymple of Orangefield, was an ardent local supporter of the bard. Burns wrote of him: *I have found a worthy warm friend* and described him in a (suppressed) stanza in *The Vision* as:

> The owner of a pleasant spot
> Near sandy wilds, I last did note
> A heart too warm, a pulse too hot
> At times o'er ran;
> But large in every feature wrote,
> Appeared the man.

Dalrymple took it upon himself to organise the bard's pony-ride to Edinburgh and armed him with a personal letter of introduction to his brother-in-law James, fourteenth Earl of Glencairn.

James was Elizabeth Maguire's second son, who had succeeded to his father's title in 1775 after the death of his elder brother. He too was a great admirer of Burns, after his factor had first called his attention to the Kilmarnock Edition of his poems (published in 1760). It was James, in company with his mother Elizabeth, the dowager Countess, who gave Burns a warm welcome and smoothed his passage into Edinburgh society.

Burns was deeply influenced by him, finding both a compassionate patron and mentor, *whose worth and brotherly kindness to me I shall remember when time will be no more.* In practical terms, Glencairn was highly instrumental in advancing Burns as a publishing poet. He introduced him to his old tutor and travelling companion, William Creech, who arranged the publication of the extended Edinburgh Edition of his poems. Underwriting its success was very much the handiwork of the Glencairns. His mother, Elizabeth, bought 124 copies, while James cajoled the gentlemen of the Caledonian Hunt *universally, one and all* to subscribe for a further hundred copies.

Even after Edinburgh had tired of Burns, and he had returned to Ayrshire and farming (May 1787), Glencairn remained his sponsor. It was to him that Burns turned to secure his appointment to the Excise Service as a riding officer along the wild coast of Dumfriesshire. Burns sought to repay his *weight of obligation* to Glencairn by composing *Verses to be written below a Noble Earl's Pictures* in his honour. This Glencairn declined.

In late January 1791 Glencairn took gravely ill after landing at Falmouth from a passage from Lisbon and died soon afterwards.

On hearing of his patron's untimely death, Burns was moved to write one of his most poignant laments, the last two stanzas of which are:

> *O! why has worth so short a date,*
> *While villains ripen grey with time?*
> *Must thou, the noble, gen'rous, great,*
> *Fall in bold manhood's hardy prime*
> *Why did I live to see that day –*
> *A day to me so full of woe?*
> *O! had I met the mortal shaft*
> *That laid my benefactor low.*
>
> *The bridegroom may forget his bride*
> *Was made his wedded wife yestreen:*
> *The monarch may forget the crown*
> *That on his head an hour has been:*
> *The mother may forget the child*
> *That smiles sae sweetly on her knee;*
> *But I'll remember thee, Glencairn*
> *And a' that thou hast done for me!*

In that year Glencairn's brother-in-law, James Dalrymple, was declared bankrupt and the Orangefield estate sold to meet his creditors. So ended the influence of Macrae's legacy on Scottish culture. The name Glencairn, however, lived on, as Burns christened his fourth son (born January 1794) James Glencairn Burns in memory of his patron.

CHAPTER 2

Lord Archibald Hamilton & the Pirates of New Providence

Captain Macrae's experiences at the hands of pirates were not unique. There are many reports of piratical acts of violence lodged by hard-pressed Scottish mariners around this period.

Virtually all of the incidents led directly back to the dispersal of the great pirate nest of New Providence in the Bahamas in 1718. This scattering of more than two thousand pirates across the trade routes of the world could not have come at a worse time for Scotland's merchant classes. The boom following the Act of Union of 1707 was short-lived and largely over by the time the Jacobite Rebellion of 1715 halted all overseas trade. It took a few years thereafter for the tobacco and sugar merchants, operating mainly out of the Clyde, to recover their nerve. Their vessels started heading west again just as the virus of Black Flag piracy was spreading out of control across the Atlantic Ocean and beyond.

This phenomenon was, ironically, a direct result of the British government's new initiative aimed at stamping out the scourge of piracy in Caribbean waters. Piracy had flourished under the cover of legitimate privateering against Spain and France, the enemies of the Protestant William of Orange and later Queen Anne. As William Bignall despairingly wrote in 1709 from Jamaica:

> Privateers may follow anyone of our own ships out of port, and take away what he sees good and burn the ship, and we never the wiser. It is the opinion of every one this cursed trade will breed so many pirates, that when peace comes we shall be in more danger from them that we are now from the enemy, their captains have no command, every man is allowed to vote, and so most votes carry the vessell where they please.

His assessment was prophetic, for when a general peace with France and Spain was declared in 1713, piratical attacks on British vessels and townships of the outlying colonies surged.

The explosion of piracy in the Caribbean, however, was largely triggered by the actions of Lord Archibald Hamilton of Riccartoun (Linlithgow). He was the seventh son of the third Duke of Hamilton. As a most faithful servant of Queen Anne, he had made his name as the captain of HMS *Litchfield* while defending Orkney and Shetland waters from attack by Jacobite and French privateers. While discharging his duty, Hamilton had netted a considerable amount of prize money. He then rose rapidly through the ranks of the English (British after 1707) navy to become Governor of Jamaica, a position he secured under the patronage of his uncle, George, Earl of Orkney.

On his arrival at Kingston, in 1711, Hamilton clashed head-on with the old gang of vested interests who had previously dominated the island's ruling council. Hamilton's first act was to weed them out from positions of authority. Their leader, the resident Chief Justice, Peter Heywood, proved impossible to oust. Up until then, he and his cronies had greatly benefited from privateering raids on the Spanish and French colonies and shipping. After over twenty years of continuous warfare, it had become an ingrained way of life with the seafaring fraternity.

Such was the reputation of their privateers that by 1712 Spain had suspended the annual shipment of plate (gold and silver) – the *flotta* – from the New World, as the 'tit-for-tat' war at sea between the Spanish and British colonists still raged unchecked. By 1715 there were three years of deferred bullion shipments stockpiled at Cartagena and Vera Cruz, awaiting escort across the Atlantic.

Hamilton's extensive and costly spy network was quick to report the sailing of the two richest plate fleets of the century. First into Havana was the Cartagena fleet with its consignment of silver and gold coins from the Colombian mint, Peruvian gold jewellery (from an Inca King's ransom), and 166 chests of emeralds from the mines of Muzo. A late addition to its cargo manifest was a wedding gift of sumptuous jewels, ordered by King Phillip V for his new bride, Elizabeth Farnese, the Duchess of Parma.

On 26 April 1715, as the last of the eight chests of this present was stowed on the Commodore's flagship, Hamilton wrote to the Admiralty in London under a *Most Secret cover: By late advices from Havana I am told the galleons from Vera Cruz were dayly Expected there in order to join the Spanish ships of war, who are said to have great Treasure on board for Old Spain.* His intelligence was correct as, shortly afterwards, the Vera Cruz fleet arrived heavily laden with gold and silver ingots from the Mexico City mint, along with silks, ivory and porcelain from Canton and Manila. These latter cargoes had been delivered across the Pacific to Acapulco, and then ferried overland by pack mule to Vera Cruz.

Hamilton's heavy hints at this once-in-a-lifetime opportunity to plunder the coffers of Spain were ignored by their Lordships sitting in London. They firmly refused to condone any act of aggression that would break the fragile peace in Europe. There was also the delicate matter of the British Court being in official mourning for the recently deceased Spanish Queen. Hamilton was, therefore, forced by circumstance to curb his avaricious instincts and assume the role of passive bystander.

On 24 July 1715 the Spanish plate *flotta* of twelve galleons, accompanied by heavily armed escorts, sailed out in fine weather and unmolested past Havana's Le Morro fortress. In overall command was General Don Estebano de Ulvelia, Knight of St James. Nine days later, in the Florida Straits, a hurricane smashed into the fleet, catching all but one galleon too close inshore to work out to sea. Once stranded on the reefs and shoals, they faced a certain wrecking as mountainous seas, whipped by hundred-knot winds, crashed onto the decks – *so violent that the water flew in the air like arrows, do[ing] injury to those it hit* – tearing away masts and superstructure.

On that terrible night, ten vessels were sunk and over a thousand men drowned. The hundreds of survivors who managed to scramble ashore amidst the wreckage faced further tribulations from hostile native Indians and their own callous commanders. Two long boats were salvaged and sent north and south to raise the alarm. The Spanish military authorities at St Augustine (Georgia) were the first to respond. Its governor sent a party of infantry with orders to summarily execute – which they did – any survivor found with so much as one looted coin on his person. With them were priests whose primary function was to hear the last confession of the condemned men.

Small naval units were also brought up to stand guard over the wrecks, eight of which were lying in the shallows amidst the reefs. As this was shark-infested water, a local Indian tribe was enslaved to provide divers. They were forced to use upturned weighted barrels as air bells. None survived the ordeal. By such methods, however, a fifth of the treasure was officially accounted for by the end of the year.

Despite all attempts at secrecy, news of the wrecking of the plate *flotta* soon reached Hamilton's ear back in Jamaica. By November he had commissioned, in partnership with a group of Port Royal merchants, three small private men-of-war. These were the snow *Eagle* (Captain Wills) and the sloops *Bersheba* (Captain Jennings) and *Bennet* (Captain Fernando). They departed *carrying more than eight hundred Men fitted out in Warlike manner, doubly provided with Grenados and bombs* under the cover story that they were hunting *Spanish pyrates*.

Since the declaration of peace, Spanish armed vessels had seized more than forty Jamaican vessels under the pretence that they were interloping traders caught within five leagues of their shores. Indeed, Hamilton had received a deputation of Jamaican merchants who delivered a petition demanding that their trade and vessels be given armed protection to replace the naval warships that were being recalled back to Britain with the peace.

Hamilton's three armed cruisers went straight to the wrecks that December. Once there, they found it easier to attack the storehouse on the shoreline for its cache of raised treasure than to dive for it themselves. According to the incensed Spanish governor of Cuba, they were barbarous robbers who overwhelmed the forty defending soldiers, then *nailed the guns and stripped the men naked* before looting the small fort.

The *Eagle* and the *Bersheba* returned in early January 1716 with 120,000 silver 'pieces of eight' (£27,000) forcibly seized from the Spanish guards. Matters came to a head with the return of the sloop *Bennet*. Her captain, Francis Fernando, had intercepted a Spanish vessel only eight miles off the Florida Keys, heading for Havana, and kept her as prize. On board were 49,000 salvaged 'pieces of eight' and a small fortune in cochineal and indigo dyes. Hamilton, as a part-owner of the *Bennet*, stood to gain one-third of this booty, blatantly taken in Spanish waters in peacetime.

To the Governor of Cuba and his Chamber of Commerce sitting in Havana this was a clear-cut case of piracy against Spanish nationals and His Most Catholic Majesty's property. Furthermore, it was a criminal act carried out with the apparent full knowledge and approval of the British governor sitting in Port Royal. He immediately dispatched his deputy, Don Juan Del Ville, to contest the prize case and extract full satisfaction from Hamilton.

His arrival in Kingston finally drove home to Hamilton the true extent of the compromising position into which he had got himself. In a desperate effort to protect himself he sold his shares in the three vessels, renounced his share of their booty and cancelled their quasi-naval 'pirate-hunting' commissions after just one voyage.

To deal with the immediate problem of the most recent attack made by Captain Fernando, Hamilton dispatched his trusted secretary, William Cockburn, to intercept him as he hovered off Jamaica. His instructions were that the cargo of silver and dyes was to be taken off the Spanish prize and landed on the north side of Jamaica. Only then was she to be brought round to Port Royal for condemnation before the Vice-Admiralty Court sitting at St Jago de la Vega (Spanish Town).

In an attempt to distance himself, Hamilton also refused to have any further dealings with Captain Fernando. Fernando, facing the Spanish demand that he should be hanged as a pirate, reacted angrily to being made the scapegoat. He insisted that he had acted in accordance with Hamilton's commission, as his 'Spanish prize' was, in reality, the sloop *Kensington* of Port Royal, taken by *Spanish pyrates* the previous year. Prior to that illegal seizure, she had been the property of the Receiver-General of Customs of Jamaica, Colonel Broderick, a close supporter of Heywood.

Fernando demanded an urgent meeting with Hamilton to clear his name. After three days' silence, Hamilton reluctantly agreed, on condition that Fernando came alone, at nine o'clock at night, to a secluded side door in his garden. This clandestine meeting was, however, immediately leaked back to his opponents in the island's Council. The spy in Hamilton's camp was his under secretary, William Page, who had been secretly serving as an informant to Heywood, ever since Hamilton's arrival.

Page also seems, without Hamilton's immediate knowledge, to have obliged his old friends by issuing at least ten more privateering commissions that summer. With the genie well and truly out of the bottle, the mania for treasure-hunting swept through the island. Captain Blechen, the master of a merchantman in Port Royal, later complained to the Admiralty that ten of his crew had deserted: *being all mad to go a wrecking as they term it; For the Generality of the Island think they have Right to fish upon the Wrecks, although the Spaniards have not quitted them.*

After he had unleashed this second wave of treasure-raiders, Page absented himself without leave that March, and took passage on HMS *Diamond*, returning to London. He did so on Heywood's orders as he carried dispatches to their Lordships of the Board of Trade. These contained signed testimonies as to Hamilton's reckless actions and personal profiteering at the expense of the peace with Spain.

In this way the blame for the recent outrages was laid at Hamilton's doorstep. One such deposition – that of Captain Jonathan Barner of the snow *Tiger* – solemnly swore that Governor Hamilton had known of his new commission. Indeed, it was Hamilton, he claimed, who had personally instructed him to go to the wrecks and *take the money out of the water, if they were stronger than the Spanish*. The other key witnesses were the Deputy Governor of Cuba, Del Ville, and the Chief Justice of Jamaica, Heywood.

The outcome of all this skulduggery was that the un-suspecting Hamilton was summarily dismissed from his post by Royal Command late that summer. In his place as governor was appointed the now favoured Peter Heywood. On receiving his appointment Heywood lost no time. Hamilton was arrested and within days dispatched as a prisoner to face trial in London.

Once there, Hamilton was granted bail to prepare his defence. His case was to be heard before their Lordships of the Board of Trade. He was, by now, fully aware of just how easily Heywood and his cronies had outmanoeuvred him with the help of Page. Belatedly, he penned and published a spirited defence: *An Answer to the Anonymous Libel; entitled Articles & Exhibits against Lord Archibald Campbell*, which was circulated in London.

In it he denounced his accusers as *a set of violent and ill-designing men*. Page, he claimed, had acted directly against his explicit order that no further passes should be issued for voyages to the wrecks. Indeed, it was Page who had wilfully forged more, for his own nefarious ends, by misappropriating some old blank commissions that Hamilton had signed prior to his declaration. He cited the minutes of the Council of Jamaica to prove that he had issued only three such passes. These were granted with the strict understanding that they might dive on the wrecks for plate, if the immediate sea area was uncontested by Spanish guard ships.

He had a strong case, and, as none of his accusers chose to respond or make an appearance, he was acquitted of all charges due to insufficient evidence. The damage, however, had been done and he did not receive his office back. Heywood, whilst escaping immediate censure, fared no better, as he was soon replaced as governor. Only the duplicitous Page was singled out by the Board and labelled a man who should never again be given a position of trust.

Just before his arrest, one of Hamilton's last acts as governor was to declare the passes, illicitly issued by Page to the second wave of treasure hunters, null and void. Henceforth, any captain who attacked and pillaged a Spanish vessel or fort in peacetime was a pirate, and would be treated as such.

The *cause célèbre* was the case of Captain Henry Jennings on the *Bersheba*. Jennings had sailed to the wrecks for a third time under the direct orders of the new owner of the sloop, Daniel De Costa Alvarenga, a Jewish merchant in Kingston. Hamilton, now alert to the actions of Page, had used all his authority to try and stop the *Bersheba* sailing, but this was ignored.

When Jennings reappeared off Port Royal he had on board 30,000 'pieces of eight', forcibly taken at sea from a Spanish vessel that he had intercepted as it returned from the salvage site. Hamilton made it abundantly clear that, should the *Bersheba* enter

Kingston harbour, the sloop and her cargo would be impounded and her captain arrested. Faced with the dilemma of giving up his stolen fortune or facing a capital charge of piracy, Jennings and his crew chose to sail away with their booty.

By then the security situation over the wrecks had deteriorated to a state of lawlessness. Bermudan sloops had muscled-in without procuring a pass from Hamilton's office. Worse still, the Brethren of the Coast turned up in their droves. When not pirating, these freebooters made a dubious living as dyewood loggers along the hotly disputed 'Mosquito Coast' (Belize and Honduras) and the Bay of Campechy (Mexico). They owed little allegiance to any authority and set about the wanton pillaging of the Spanish forts and vessels along the Florida coast to acquire bullion and munitions.

Spanish retaliation was not long in coming and they launched a punitive raid on the Brethren's encampments. At one location in the Bay of Campechy, twelve vessels were burned, along with onshore huts and stores. Those crews and loggers not slaughtered fled into the jungle where they were left to face starvation. It was, therefore, an easy step for them to turn (or return in some cases) to piracy and start looting ships of any nationality they encountered in order to replenish their provisions.

Forcibly evicted from the mainland, most followed Captain Jennings' example and headed for Avery's old pirate haunt of New Providence in the Bahamas. This island, after the Spanish and French raids of 1700, was virtually uninhabited and had momentarily slipped from the immediate control or interest of the British Crown.

This gathering had not gone unnoticed. The Earl of Orkney's proxy governor of Virginia, the Scot, James Spottiswood, wrote to London in July 1716: *a nest of pirates are endeavouring to establish themselves in New Providence and by the additions they expect, and will probably receive, of loosely disordered people from the Bay of Campechy, Jamaica and other parts, may prove dangerous to the British commerce, if not timely suppressed.*

It was a prophetic warning for, during the next few months, two thousand of the Brethren moved to the island. Their sprawling encampment soon turned the shoreline of the main anchorage into an open cesspit, the stench from which was detectable many miles out to sea.

The natural prey of these pirates was the square-rigged brigs and ships that exploited the 'great circle' of the North Atlantic trade winds that took them out of Caribbean waters via the Florida Straits. The location of the Bahamas as a base for piracy was, therefore, ideal. Their small fast raiders, led by a galaxy of pirate captains, soon swarmed all over this sea area, taking any vessel heading for the North American seaboard or Europe. When not chasing plate galleons and rich merchantmen they turned to looting the smaller craft in the inter-island trade for provisions and marine stores.

The security situation in the Caribbean rapidly became so grave that the governors of the sugar islands were sternly predicting the collapse of the whole plantation economy, as few vessels reached Europe or America without the protection of a convoy. An immediate and comprehensive solution was, therefore, needed.

In the summer of 1717 the Privy Council met at Hampton Court to deliberate on this matter. There was, by then, a much greater sense of urgency as the mounting pirate attacks on neutral vessels were creating diplomatic tensions that threatened the peace in Europe.

The outcome of their deliberations was *A Proclamation for the Suppressing of Pirates*, which resurrected a tried and tested 'carrot and stick' strategy. The 'carrot' was a pardon, the Act of Grace, for any pirate who would forswear his criminal ways and return to lawful pursuits by a set date. The offer of pardon was, given the distances involved, valid for a year after receiving the royal assent.

This Act was, however, fatally compromised by the ludicrous decision to include a four-month additional deferment from when an individual's piratical activity might be reported: *We do hereby promise and declare, that in case any of the said pirates shall on or before 5th September in the year of our Lord 1718 surrender themselves ... shall have our gracious pardon of ... their piracies committed before 5th January next.*

This royal proclamation duly arrived safely at New Providence from Bermuda on board HMS *Phoenix* in early December. What happened next was farcical. Three hundred pirates presented themselves for pardon, knowing full well that they had the best part of a month in which to continue raiding. The more belligerent held out for a further extension in which to pursue their interests and dispose of their stock of looted goods. Indeed, they went so far as to threaten to forcibly take over the isolated island of Bermuda and turn it into a 'new Madagascar' if refused.

The 'stick' was a small naval force under the direction of Sir Woodes Rogers who, by a Royal Commission, was appointed the first *Captain-General and Governor-in-Chief in and over our Bahamas islands in America*. The redoubtable Rogers was very much the 'poacher turned gamekeeper' as he was one of the most famous captains of his time. As a privateering commander he had circumnavigated the globe in his pursuit of Spanish bullion which culminated in the taking of the *Acapulco* galleon on its annual passage across the Pacific. He had actively petitioned the Court to be given this appointment, but with the condition that he would have a free hand in dealing with his unruly Bahamian subjects – many of whom were his old shipmates.

He appeared off New Providence in July 1718 on the ex-East Indiaman *Delicia* (460 ton), accompanied by his own trading sloop, the *Buck*. Escorting them was a pirate-hunting naval force comprising the 32-gun fifth-rater HMS *Milford*, the 20-gun sixth-rater HMS *Rose* and the 10-gun sloop-of-war *Shark*.

The arrival of such a powerful force had been anticipated by a number of the more die-hard pirate companies. Those following Edward 'Blackbeard' Teach, Major Stede Bonnet, Christopher Condent and 'Calico' Jack Rackham had already slipped away north to raid along the coast of mainland America. Edward England led those crossing the Atlantic to plunder the shipping and slaving forts of the Guinea Coast of West Africa.

Their ringleader, Charles Vane, was still in New Providence. He sent out a letter to Rogers as his flotilla entered Bahamian waters, demanding an extension to the date for the royal pardon and a free hand with their loot. Rogers was determined not to start his governorship by make any such deals, as he had a powerful naval force at his disposal. Accordingly, he sent one escort to each entrance of the New Providence Channel to block Vane's escape.

Vane's response was to send a French prize full of munitions as a fire ship down the East Channel that night. He almost succeeded in ensnaring the *Rose*, forcing her captain to slip his cable and run out to sea. Foiled in his design, Vane exploited the mayhem of blazing tar barrels and exploding gunpowder casks to clear out the unguarded channel and vanish into the darkness. He left behind a note swearing to return to burn out Rogers once his naval protectors had left. The old hands watching on dry land as bystanders chose the less dramatic 'wait and see' policy.

Three days later Rogers landed with a number of settlers and a small group of soldiers, complete with a chest of Bibles provided by the Society for the Propagation of Christian Knowledge for his pirate flock. He was greeted by a 'guard of honour' headed by two pirate captains, Benjamin Hornigold and Thomas Burgess. They had organised some 300 drunken inhabitants into two lines who fired volleys wildly into the air, whilst cheering King George.

He described his arrival in a letter to the Lords Commissioners for Trade and Plantations:

> Your Lordships,
>
> I arriv'd in this Port on the 26 July last in company with the Men of Warr ordered to assist me. I met with little opposition in coming in, but found a French ship (that was taken by the Pirates of 22 Guns) burning in the Harbour ... which we were told was set on Fire to drive out His Majestys Ship the Rose who got in too early the evening before me, and cut her cable and run out in the Night for fear of being burnt by one Charles Vane who command'd the Pirates and at our [approach] and His Majesty's Ship the Milford near approach the next morning, they finding it impossible to escape us, he with about ninety men fled away in a Sloop wearing the black Flag and Fir'd guns of Defiance when they perceiv'd their Sloop out Sayl'd the Two that I sent to chase them hence

Rogers wasted no time in fortifying the two entrances against the return of Vane and his likes. A number of the 600 old lags who had taken the pardon since his arrival, including Olivier 'La Bouche', were provided with strong liquor as an inducement to labour alongside the soldiers rebuilding the ruined bastions of the old forts. A council was convened and law officers appointed from among the settlers and a few trusted indigenous inhabitants. Things were going well for Rogers, and his vision of a self-sufficient, productive and ordered plantation seemed within his grasp. Unfortunately, a terrible fever swept the island, decimating his new settlers and the crews of the naval ships in the anchorage.

He was acutely aware that time was not on his side, especially as his naval commanders were anxious to clear out to sea to avoid the sickness. With the prospect of a new war with Spain over Gibraltar looming, these commanders needed little excuse to abandon their policing role at New Providence which kept them from earning high fees as convoy escorts.

By late summer they had gone, leaving Rogers with only the *Delicia* and the *Buck*. Without a naval presence to intimidate them, hundreds of the Brethren drifted back to their old habits. Rogers struggled to find other schemes to occupy their more aggressive talents. The prospect of a new conflict with Spain provided what seemed a perfect diversion for the malcontents under his charge.

With this in mind, he fitted two armed sloops, the *Buck* and the *Mumvil Trader*, as privateers for a 'forced trading' mission to Spanish Hispaniola. They sailed under his hand-picked captains, Brisk and Porter, each with a complement of some thirty hands recruited from the cream of the pardoned pirates.

Their unwelcome visit to 'Privateers Bay' only netted a few low-value prizes. As they disembarked their European goods and supplies to trade for contraband colonial goods with the locals, seven disgruntled veteran buccaneers from the *Buck* made their move. They seized Captain Brisk, the surgeon, Doctor Murray, and the first mate at pistol point, while they were consulting in the aft cabin. Soon afterwards an element of the crew on the other sloop also seized their officers. In pirate fashion, they elected their ringleader and 'foremast man', the Welshman Howell Davis, as their captain. The six Blades that first stood by him were Walter Kennedy, Thomas Antis, Dennis Topping (Toppen), Richard Jones, Roger Hughes (Hews) and John Clerk.

Davis immediately ordered the raising of the Black Flag, thereby abandoning all pretence of chasing only Spanish prizes. The deposed captains, their first mates and a few faint-hearted and sickly mariners were unceremoniously dumped on a French vessel after it had been looted off Barbados. The Scots surgeon and the rest of the two crews were detained on board the *Buck*.

Freed from all constraints, Davis turned north to raid for a while off the western coast of Dominica. There he took a few American vessels and two from New Providence. A number of the crews from the latter port decided to join him.

By that time, however, Governor Rogers was back in full control of New Providence, having caught and hanged a few backsliders in front of hundreds of their old comrades. Howell Davis, standing on the deck of the Governor's own sloop, knew for certain that Rogers would now send out his new 'game-keepers', Hornigold and Burgess, to hunt him down, should he stay in Caribbean waters. And so Davis set the *Buck* eastwards, out into the vast expanse of the Atlantic.

Weeks later he arrived off the Isle of May in the Cape Verde Islands off West Africa. By this fine piece of navigation, he had brought the *Buck* safely to a small remote island that was a well-frequented watering place and source of natural salt for vessels bound for the West Indies or the Indian Ocean.

At his leisure, and in sight of the local mayor, he plundered a number of vessels for stores before deciding to keep a large Liverpool merchantman as his new flagship. Cocking his snook at the Georgian establishment he renamed her the *King James*. With the *Buck* as escort, he then headed south for the West African coast and the rich pickings around the slaving forts.

They made landfall off the St James Fort on the Gambia River. Davis's audacious plan was to scout out the garrison's defences before attacking. To do this he posed, along with the first mate and the doctor, as enquiring gentleman officers. Well received by the local governor, they were invited to dine. At the table Davis drew a hidden brace of pistols and overpowered the host and his staff. He then fired a shot through an open window as the signal for twenty waiting pirates to rush the guard-room. With the fort in their hands they found out, to their dismay, that they had just missed a gold shipment. In their frustration they sacked the fort for what they could carry and set it ablaze.

As they were about to clear out to sea, they ran into the Frenchman La Bouche who had, like so many from New Providence, reneged on his pardon and turned pirate before crossing over to Africa. The two companies, after a two-day drinking session, made a pact to cruise together. The *Buck* was abandoned where she lay and her crew was transferred to the *King James*. This gave them the necessary force to attack another fort with less risk. Their chosen target was the isolated English Royal Africa Company fort on Bance Island, a few miles up the Sierra Leone River.

As they worked their way up this great estuary, they fell in with yet another New Providence brother, the lethally mercurial Thomas Cocklyn, who was busy looting the *Bird* galley of Bristol.

With a flotilla of three ships and hundreds of armed men at their disposal, they made their move on Bance Island fort. This neglected outpost of the Royal Africa Company fell after a day and a night of bombardment and a determined assault by a landing party. The last of the defenders fled upriver in canoes, leaving the fort open to the pirates who plundered it before putting it to the torch.

As fate would have it, the pirates settled down for a well-earned seven-week carousal and refit at 'Old Crackers' settlement at the mouth of the Sierra Leone River, just as the Clyde's first generation of dedicated slavers were arriving off the Guinea Coast. The clash of two vested interests was destined to alter the entire direction of Glasgow's emerging entrepreneurial aspirations.

As for the pirates, their cycle of violence would terminate a year later. For most the end was the gallows outside the gates of Cape Coast (Corso) Castle, Ghana. Of a splinter group led by Walter Kennedy, two would be murdered by locals along a desolate Argyllshire road, and nine of their number hanged – including 'Lords' Hughes, Jones and Clerk – between the low and high water marks on the Sands of Leith.

CHAPTER 3

Robert Louis Stevenson
& the Pirates

Treasure Island, first published as a book in 1883, catapulted Robert Louis Stevenson onto the world stage as an author of adventure stories. The spur to write this timeless masterpiece of storytelling was drawing a map of the island for the amusement for Lloyd Osborne, the young son of his American wife Fanny, on a wet day in Braemar during the summer of 1881.

The tale (first entitled *The Sea Cook*) has the last of the New Providence 'gentlemen of fortune', led by the immortal Long John Silver, as the most memorable of characters. The pirate's name was borrowed from the owner (Juan Silverado) of a remote bunkhouse in the mountains behind the Napa Valley of California where he and Fanny had spent their honeymoon the previous year. Stevenson freely confessed to modelling the personality of Silver on his close friend and collaborator William Henley, who had lost a foot to tuberculosis of the bone:

> *It was the sight of your maimed strength and masterfulness that begot John Silver. Of course he is not in any other quality or feature the least like you:*

but the idea of the maimed man ruling and dreaded by the sound, was entirely from you.

Henley contributed greatly to the tale, which was written at breakneck speed, by sending books on pirates up to Braemar. There, Stevenson, bedridden for most of the day, devoured them. He later told his agent, *T. I. came out of Kingsley's At Last; where I got the 'Dead Man's Chest' – and that was the seed – and out of the great Captain Johnson's* History of Notorious Pyrates.

In the latter he found the peg-legged saviour of Captain Macrae on the *Cassandra* – the historical match for his blood-soaked old pirate Silver. In a close parallel to the Macrae story, he has Silver save Hawkins from pirate bloodlust, by the dramatic intervention, *I've never seen a better boy than that ... let me see him that'll lay a hand on him – that's what I say, and you may lay to it.*

Earlier in the plot, the fifty-year-old Silver refers to his time as a pirate on the *Cassandra* when recruiting new hands to his latest mutiny – unaware that Hawkins was hiding in the apple barrel:

Flint was cap'n; I was quartermaster, along with my timber leg. The same broadside I lost my leg, old Pew lost his dead-lights. It was a master surgeon, him that ampytated me – out of college and all – Latin by the bucket, and what not; but he was hanged like a dog, and sun-dried like the rest, at Corso Castle. That was Roberts's men, that was, and comed of changing names to their ships Royal Fortune *and so on. Now, what a ship was christened, so let her stay, I says. So it was with the* Cassandra, *as brought us safe home from Malabar, after England took the* Viceroy of the Indies; *so it was with the old* Walrus, *Flint's old ship, as I've seen a-muck with the red blood and fit to sink with gold ... Davis was a man, too, by all accounts ... I never sailed with him; first England, then with Flint, that's my story.*

Stevenson had, of course, switched round the name of the treasure ship from the *Nostra Senhro de Cabo* to that of its Portuguese owner – the *Viceroy of the Indies* – as one eminently more suited to an Anglo-Saxon audience. Flint was probably modelled on England's consort, the ruthless John Taylor, and hence the old *Walrus* is the old *Victory* in Johnson's *Pyrates*.

Stevenson also borrowed other characters from the same source. Israel 'Basilica' Hands sailed with Edward 'Blackbeard' Teach who shot him through the kneecap with a pistol under the table during a drinking bout. Stevenson was, no doubt, unable to resist deploying such a wonderful name and its association with the extremes of pirate cruelty.

The character of the marooned Ben Gunn is taken straight out of Defoe's *Robinson Crusoe*. Indeed, Stevenson initially penned the character as chasing goats and dressed in their skins. But at the first evening reading of this new chapter in Braemar both stepson Lloyd and father Thomas Stevenson protested that the character was blatantly a take-off of Crusoe. Consequently, the goats were dropped and Gunn's attire changed to *tatters of ship's canvas and old sea cloth*.

Stevenson displays his new-found mastery of pirate history when he first raises the spectre of the bygone Golden Age of Piracy in the tale. The vehicle is the feathery Captain Flint – Silver's parrot:

> *And that bird ... is, may be two hundred years old, Hawkins – they lives for ever mostly; and if anybody's seen more wickedness, it must be the devil himself. She sailed with England, the great Cap'n England, the pirate. She's*

been at Madagascar, and at Malabar, and Surinam, and Providence, and Portobello. She was at the fishing up of the wrecked Plate ships. It's there she learned 'Pieces of eight', and little wonder; three hundred and fifty thousand of 'em, Hawkins! She was at the boarding of the Viceroy of the Indies out of Goa, she was; and to look at her you would think she was a babby. But you smelt powder – didn't you, cap'n.

Stevenson's description of Flint's buried treasure fits that plundered in the Indian Ocean rather than the Caribbean: *a strange collection ... English, French, Spanish, Portuguese, Georges and Louises, doubloons and moidores and sequins ... Oriental pieces stamped with what looked like wisps of string or bits of spider's web, round pieces and square pieces, and pieces bored through the middle ...*

He acknowledged that he got the idea of buried treasure from reading Edgar Allan Poe's *The Gold Bug* (1824). This short story was based on the legend of Blackbeard's loot buried on Sullivan's Island in the entrance to Charleston harbour. The hoard was located by a dead-man's skull in a tree, a device that Stevenson transformed to a stretched out human skeleton on the ground in *Treasure Island*.

It is, however, well nigh impossible to determine where Stevenson's island is. In the story, the young Hawkins's deliberately strikes out the island's longitude and latitude in his copy of Billy Bones's map. Likewise, he simply passes over, in a few words, the voyages to and from the island. His explanation is that Flint's hoard of silver is still buried on the island. This masterstroke of storytelling, along with the disappearance of Silver at an unnamed port on the Spanish Main, leaves the tale as but one episode in a murky saga of unfinished pirate business, stretching back through thirty-odd years of violent crimes committed across half the globe.

Stevenson steadfastly refused to give as much as a hint as to the island's location. A crafty reporter from the *Sydney Morning Herald* tried to corner him on this matter, in February 1890, with a sneaky adjoiner to a lead question: *I suppose that you will utilise your experience in the South Sea in your next work of fiction? By the by, did you visit Treasure Island?* Stevenson wryly smiled at this ploy and palmed him off with: *Treasure Island is not in the Pacific. In fact, I only wish myself that I knew where it was. When I wrote the book I was careful to give no indication as to its whereabouts, for fear that there might be an undue rush towards it. However, it is generally supposed to be in the West Indies. But to be serious …* At which point he changed the subject to a new plot he was working on.

Local Scottish tradition has the last word. It holds that Stevenson loosely based the physical layout of Treasure Island on the horseshoe islet of Fidra in the Firth of Forth. This claim is founded on the fact that he visited that island as a youth, when his father was building the lighthouse there and he later used this location in his Scottish novel *Catriona*.

CHAPTER 4

The Pirates of Craignish Loch

On the evening of 9 February 1720 Lady Campbell of Barbreck House, at the head of the remote Loch Craignish in Argyllshire, opened her door to two strangers of wild appearance. They claimed they were seamen sent by the captain of the 100-ton snow, *Flying Eagle* of Dartmouth, that was lying to her anchors five miles down the loch. She had been blown into this sea-loch in great distress by a gale while en route to Newfoundland and the fisheries. Their enquiry was not for food or shelter but whether or not there was a magistrate in the immediate vicinity. On hearing that the nearest resided in Inveraray, some forty miles by unimproved drove road round the coast, they took their leave.

It was never recorded what raised Lady Campbell's suspicions to the degree that she felt she must send her son, by the shortest possible route directly over the mountains in midwinter, to summon help from Inveraray. These were certainly dangerous times in the West Highlands. Indeed, it was just over a year since the Spanish had landed hundreds of soldiers at Loch Duich, further up the coast, in a forlorn attempt to foment another rebellion on behalf of the 'Old Pretender'.

Suffice it to say that these seamen – whether Jacobites or pirates – had the gross misfortune to have landed in Campbell territory. This was a staunchly Hanoverian area and a bastion of government law and order in the otherwise lawless region.

Her son, accompanied by a servant, safely reached Inveraray. This was the seat of the Duke of Argyll and the only town of consequence for ninety miles around. There they were ushered in front of the resident Sheriff Depute for Argyllshire, James Campbell of Stonefield. Their tale came hard behind recent reports of drunken strangers causing trouble on the shore road along Loch Fyne. This new piece of information provided Stonefield with the ultimate source of his problem.

Even as he was assembling an armed mounted posse, a group of ruffians entered a hostelry in Inveraray. Suspicions were fully aroused when this rabble paid for their strong liquor with Portuguese gold coins. On Stonefield's orders, the men were immediately arrested. Over the next few days more suspects were rounded-up heading for Greenock and marched off to join their comrades in Inveraray's small jailhouse.

Most were found laden with gold coins and treasure hidden about their persons. All in all, Stonefield impounded some 3,000 Portuguese moidores, 2,000 English guineas, 200 ounces of gold dust and over £5,000 worth of assorted jewellery and trinkets.

Stonefield then set about interrogating his prisoners. As a trained advocate, it took him only three sessions to destroy their cover story of being distressed seamen bound for Newfoundland on the *Flying Eagle* of Dartmouth. A number confessed to being reluctant pirates – forced men – off the *Eagle* of New York. This small snow, they divulged, had been taken while en route from

Barbados for Virginia with bread, pork and other provisions. She was now lying to her anchors in Craignish Loch.

At the first sight of the Stonefield's galloping posse charging round the head of the loch, those pirates still left on board the *Eagle* panicked. Cutting her cables, they made a frantic bid to escape out to sea, only to run her hard aground on the rocks off the ruins of the old castle that had been built to fend off the Scandinavian pirates of an earlier era. Stuck fast, her crew abandoned her.

When Stonefield's men clambered on board the *Eagle*, she was listing heavily and in imminent danger of sinking. He immediately called off the pursuit of the fleeing pirates and put his men to work salvaging the *Eagle* and her perishable cargo. His first need was to organise a round-the-clock on board watch to deter the local pilferers. After this Stonefield rode back to Inveraray to recruit carpenters to repair her badly holed hull.

With that done, he set about separating the victims of this piratical attack – the members of the *Eagle*'s rightful crew, from the perpetrators of this capital crime – the pirates. Greatly aiding his task was the presence of Dr Archibald Murray amongst the prisoners. He was the son of Murray of Deuchar and had been the surgeon on board Woodes Rogers' *Buck* of New Providence when Howell Davis seized her and turned pirate off Hispaniola. That was back in the summer of 1718 and he had, he claimed, been held captive ever since.

No doubt acting on his information, Captain James McIntosh of the *Eagle* and five of his crew were identified and released. Murray also confirmed that half the pirate crew, led by the Irishman Walter Kennedy, had got away south. Defoe, writing only five years later, states that two of them got so badly drunk on the way that they became separated from their group. They were later found murdered and stripped of their loot and clothing by the side of the track.

Back in Inveraray Jail, Stonefield was left with twenty-one battle-hardened Black Flag pirates on his hands. He knew that his isolated little prison would not hold them for long, especially as a large number of their comrades were still at large. He decided, therefore, to send them south to the more secure Tolbooth in Glasgow, some ninety miles away. This long, difficult and dangerous march got under way at the first sign of spring. The terrain they had to pass through was very rugged, and frequented at that time by the outlaw at large, Rob Roy Macgregor. The mission was accomplished without losing a prisoner.

By now the agents of central government were fully aware of the magnitude of the crimes that these prisoners had committed. As their acts of piracy had been committed outside Scottish sovereign waters and against the vessels, property and persons of other nations, it was deemed necessary to try them under the 'Law of Nations'. The most competent court to hear their case was, therefore, the High Court of Admiralty of Scotland sitting at the old Tolbooth in Edinburgh.

And so a squadron of dragoons was dispatched in late May to escort the prisoners, in chains, the forty-five miles from Glasgow to the dungeons of Edinburgh Castle. There they lay incarcerated for six months whilst the case against them was prepared. By this time two had turned King's Evidence while another two disappear from the records. They may have either died or possibly been released due to lack of evidence.

The pleas of the remaining seventeen were heard on Friday 3 November 1720. Twelve days later their trial began, presided over by Lord James Graham, acting on behalf of the Earl of Rothes, the titular Vice-Admiral of Scotland. Such a high-profile case attracted the rising young stars of the Scottish legal profession. The young and newly appointed Lord Advocate, Robert Dundas of Arniston, led the prosecution team. He was ably assisted by the Procurator Fiscal to the Admiralty Court, Sir Patrick Grant. The nine defence lawyers were led by the formidable Charles Erskine of Barjarg, first Professor of Public Law at Edinburgh University, Advocate and Member of Parliament for Dumfriesshire.

From the outset Arniston was adamant that the *Pannell* (the accused) were all *standard pirates*. Indeed, three of them – Roger Hughes (or Hews), John Clerk and Richard Jones – were pirate 'Lords'. These men, the jury was informed, were the aristocrats of piracy by virtue of their origins in the pirates' nest on the island of New Providence.

In making his case to the jury, he sought to pre-empt the anticipated defence that they were *forced men* who had only recently escaped from their captors with the intention of surrendering themselves at the first opportunity. Had this been the case, Arniston argued, they should immediately have turned themselves over to Captain McIntosh, the lawful master of the *Eagle*. By retaining control of this small snow, changing her name and painting the British coat-of-arms on her stern, they had exposed their true intention. That was to slip unnoticed into a remote part of the Irish or mainland British coast with their immense booty. Only an Act of God – the storm that blew them off course and into Loch Craignish – had foiled this scheme for their retirement from piracy.

The accused, he proclaimed, were cut-throats who had freely served under a succession of infamous pirate captains:

Howell Davis, Thomas Cocklyn, Olivier La Bouche, and finally the bloodiest of them all, Bartholomew Roberts. Over the past two years they had taken part in the most devastating raids in the annals of pirate history. They were party to the sacking and burning of a number of forts along the West African coast and the illegal taking and plundering of hundreds of vessels, both there and in South American and Caribbean waters.

During these piratical acts they had been actively involved in the murder of hundreds of people whose names and the circumstances of whose deaths would never be known. For it was the pirate way, as Arniston explained to the jury, to kill (*dead men tell no tales*) those who might later testify against them. The prosecution therefore could cite only one specific incident of murder – that of nine Africans – for their consideration. Conviction for this single act of barbarism alone would be sufficient to incur the death sentence.

This atrocity happened when the accused were crew on the flotilla led by Howell, La Bouche and Cocklyn, then cruising off the coast of Guinea. As Arniston recounted to the jury, they took these unfortunate Africans and *kept [them] in irons that night and next day hang[ed] them by the feet to the yard arm and did barbarously shote them* for target practice. To substantiate his charge that they were, indeed, bloodstained *Blades of Fortune*, Arniston offered the testament of a number of eye-witnesses. The principal witnesses to the atrocity were the forced surgeon, Archibald Murray, who had turned King's Evidence for a full pardon, and the cooper on the slaver *Loyalty* of Port Glasgow, John Daniels, who had been a prisoner of the pirates at the time.

Erskine, for the defence, acknowledged that these dreadful events had, indeed, taken place as described. However, his clients were all forced men who were not in a position to intervene without incurring the gravest risk to their own lives. They could only stand by as silent witnesses to such acts of wanton savagery.

He claimed that each of the accused had also been the victim of unbridled pirate violence. From the moment of their capture they had to endure lengthy imprisonment in irons and mock executions for refusing to sign the Articles of Regulation which would signal that they had turned pirate with the Blades. Furthermore, a number of the accused in the dock had tried to escape, for which they were severely whipped and locked away after their recapture.

The truth was that his clients had been taken from their legally trading merchantmen by the pirates at different times along the African coast and retained because of their skills. He also claimed that they had steadfastly refused to take part in acts of piracy other than the safe navigation of the ship.

It was the Blades, led by Walter Kennedy, who took the *Eagle* off Jamaica, after which they had gone back on board their flagship, the *Royal Revenge*, and got badly drunk, leaving the defendants to mind the two vessels. It was then that his clients took their chance to escape. During the night, as the Blades slept below, they nailed up the touch holes of the pirate flagship's cannons and threw all the small arms and shot they could find overboard, after which, they scrambled over the side and onto the prize that lay alongside. It was a desperate gamble, for had a Blade appeared on deck as they made off at first light, they would have been murdered on the spot.

Their sole intention, it was claimed, was to reach a British port where they could turn themselves in to the appropriate authorities. This, Erskine claimed, was evident from their enquiry after a magistrate at the doorstep of Barbreck House, that fateful evening in Craignish Loch. Thereafter, *finding themselves in Danger, and ill treated by the highlanders; they were obliged to disperse in small Companies for their own safety.* Their capture by Stonefield and his men unfortunately forestalled this plan to surrender themselves at the first opportunity and so clear their names.

Erskine ridiculed the prosecution's case, based on alleged piratical acts that happened at some non-specific location and time against vessels and masters that could not now be identified. Tackling Arniston's claim that, as Blades, they were bound by the Articles of their brotherhood not to bear witness against another, he petitioned that three of the *least likely to be guilty* in the panel should be tried first. If they were found innocent, he asserted, they would then testify as to who were the real Blades in the dock. This they would do readily as they would no longer be living in fear for their lives, as they had been during their shared confinement in Edinburgh Castle's dungeons.

Arniston was for none of it. He had packed the fifteen-man jury with local shipmasters and Edinburgh merchants. These men could be trusted to give no credence to arguments as to what might constitute 'force', other than *immediate fear of death*, which would cause a seaman to co-operate with a pirate. He also had credible witnesses to specific events: the surgeon, the supercargo, bosun and cooper of the looted *Loyalty* of Port Glasgow and the crew of the *Eagle*. The trial lasted less than a week before the jury retired to consider their verdict.

On 22 November 1720, Lord Graham was handed the jurors' sealed note. For seven of the accused the jury found their *defences of force and fear of death and sickness proven exemplar*. They were immediately dismissed at the bar. As for the remaining ten in the dock, the jury found *by a plurality of voices ... the lybll [of piracy] proven*. On receiving their verdict, Lord Graham pronounced the statutory sentence of death by hanging on each of the accused.

Dundas departed for London to obtain the King's signature on their death warrants. The warrant for the execution of Hyman Saturly was accompanied by the judge's recommendation that, as he was only sixteen at the time of his offences, he should receive the King's Pardon. This was granted.

The executions of the remaining nine were undertaken in the time-honoured manner. The establishment's vengeance was given its full vent against these men who tempted oppressed seamen to turn pirate. It was, therefore, ordained that the two 'Lords', Roger Hughes and John Clerk, be taken first: *to the Sands of Leith within the flood mark upon the second Wednesday of December. Betwixt the hours of two and four o'clock in the afternoon and there be hanged by the neck on the Gibbet till they be dead.* Their bodies were then tarred and hung in chains so that they would reappear from beneath the waves with every receding tide for as long as the rotting corpses held together. This would serve as a grisly warning to every passing ship's company of the inevitable price of piracy.

The second batch was hanged on the first Wednesday of the New Year. All four – William Fenton, John Stewart, William Green and James Sail – went to their deaths protesting their innocence to the last. Their pleas went largely unheard for, on the same day, a rival and more ghoulish event was taking place at the Grassmarket in Edinburgh which drew away the expected thousands of spectators. This was the mutilation and execution of Nicholas Mushet of Boghall for the barbarous murder of his wife. He first suffered having his offending hand struck off by the town executioner before being hanged.

The final three convicted pirates – William Minty, Richard Luntly and 'Lord' Richard Jones – were executed the following Wednesday. Just before his death Luntly, formerly from Barbados, told his sorry tale to a hack broadsheet writer. These carrion crows of the journalist profession usually hovered around the gallows waiting to pick up the *dying last words* of the condemned criminal. This journalist, however, seems to have gained access to Luntly in Edinburgh Castle vaults while he was awaiting execution. It is quite likely that he was the 'ordinary', the minister charged with hearing their last confessions; though it is possible that he simply bribed the guards.

If Luntly's account is to be believed (the factual details are readily verifiable), he had been forced off the *Guinea Hen* when she was taken by Davis in the Gambia River early in February 1719. He could, therefore, bear full witness to a full year of plundering and murder as a reluctant member of both Davis's and later Roberts's crew. He was adamant that only 'Lords' Clerk and Jones deserved to meet their end on the gibbet on Leith Sands. The other seven (including himself) were, he insisted, innocent men who had endured extremes of cruelty at the hands of the pirates only to be sacrificed, as an example to others, by the state.

As John Stewart so bitterly put it in his *Dying Words: having landed in the West of Scotland, every Body knew how we have been treated since that time, and I might have purchast my Life, had my conscience allowed me to Comply with the Solicitation of them, who would have me appear as an Evidence against those that were as innocent as myself, but I never could think of Saving my Life at so dear a Rate.*

Only 'Lord' John Clerk admitted his guilt: *I confess that I was upon the Island of Providence when Governor Rogers came with the King's Pardon to the pirates that were there, and that I was one of those who was a pirating before I came into the Buck-Sloop.* He claimed, however, that unlike Roger Hughes, he was not one of those that took part in the insurrection led by Davis. As for the other condemned men: *I go out of this world with a heavy Heart, when I think how innocently these Poor Men must suffer.* His final act was to point the finger at the man he considered solely responsible for this terrible travesty – the 'turncoat' and star witness for the prosecution, Dr Archibald Murray: *I think they are much wronged and unjustly condemned. Sentence might very justly have passed on the Doctor and me, for he and I were long engaged in these wicked Courses. But these poor men they were taken by us and ... forced to the Working of the Ship, which if they had refused they would have been shot to Death that Moment.*

The taint of a gross miscarriage of justice did not curtail the careers of the jurists who had handled the case. All lived to a ripe old age, having served in the highest offices of their profession. The presiding Admiralty Court Judge – veteran of the infamous trial of Captain Green and the crew of the *Worcester* fifteen years earlier – retired soon afterwards and founded his own ancestral seat as Graham of Airth Castle.

Robert Dundas, who had only just received his office as Lord Advocate in time to prosecute the Craignish pirates, led a charmed career. Immediately after the trial he was made Dean of Advocates, and it is he who is credited with replacing the civil 'proven/not proven' plea and verdict with the 'guilty/not guilty' in Scots Criminal Law. In 1748 he was elevated, as Lord Arniston, to the highest position of Lord President of the Court of Session.

Sir Patrick Grant, the Procurator Fiscal in the case, was also appointed to the bench, as Lord Elchies, and raised to a Lord of Justiciary in 1737. His famous collection of cases was eventually published as *Decisions of the Court of Session* in 1813.

The defending advocate, Charles Erskine, received his knighthood and was later raised to the bench as Lord Tinwald. In 1746 he was made Lord Justice Clerk and attended the marriage of his son and successor, James, later Lord Alva, to Margaret Maguire. Captain James Macrae died in July of that year and may have lived just long enough to witness the culmination of his plan to ennoble Violer Hugh's family.

As for the gold taken from the Craignish pirates, it became the centre of a lengthy legal wrangle. Campbell of Stonefield tenaciously held onto the hoard as long as his exorbitant claims for expenses were contested by Lord Graham. His most extensive bills were for the protection and repair of the *Eagle*, which he also claimed as his by right of salvage.

She had overset soon after being abandoned. To right her, another vessel, the bark *Ann* of Campbeltown, had to be brought up and lashed to her by a great hawser that took eight men to manage. In such a remote place the repair of her hull could only be effected at low tide. It was, therefore, June before she was able to sail from Loch Craignish round the Mull of Kintyre to the Clyde under the charge of John Bethune, the Collector of Customs for Edinburgh. He also submitted a substantial claim for his services.

One of the many ironies of this case is that when she finally arrived at the quay at Greenock she was moored alongside the *Loyalty*. This was the Port Glasgow slaver that had been ransacked and stripped of her rigging by Davis, Cocklyn and La Bouche off the Guinea Coast the previous year and had only just returned to the Clyde. The anchor watchman on the *Loyalty* was the star witness, the cooper Joseph Daniels, one of three skilled men forcibly taken off her during the attack. He had escaped from their clutches and made his way back from Africa in time for the arrival of his old ship.

The Earl of Rothes also threw his hat into the cockpit by demanding, as the Vice-Admiral of Scotland, his tenth share of the treasure and the salvage value of the *Eagle*.

At the time of the trial, the New York owners of the *Eagle* had petitioned the court for the return of their vessel. Stonefield successfully countered with the claim that she would have been a total wreck had he not expended his time and money on her salvage.

Indeed, this litigation over the ownership of the seized treasure and the snow continued long after the last pirate had been hanged. Three years later, the much-fought-over snow *Eagle* was finally released from judicial control and put up for sale at Leith. This brought the prolonged litigation to an end, the cost of which was met out of the gold hoard. Who received the residue – if any remained after all the legal experts had taken their fees – is not known.

It is interesting to note that the amount of treasure recovered by Stonefield accounts for less than a third of what was known to be on the Portuguese bullion galleon *Sacrada Familia* at the time she was taken off Brazil by Roberts. It would therefore seem likely that the pirates who escaped Stonefield's men and the locals of Craignish got away with the lion's share.

After the trial no more pirates off the *Eagle* were caught in Scotland. Defoe states that their captain, Walter Kennedy, made it safely to Ireland with his cache. Thereafter, he moved to the London area where he ran a house of ill repute on the Deptford Road. When he crossed one of his mistresses who knew about his past, she turned him in to the authorities for an armed robbery.

While he was in Bridewell Prison, she tracked down Thomas Grant, the mate of one of the vessels he had looted. Grant had been held as a forced man and had been severely punished for attempted escape before he finally got away. The avenging mate needed little prompting to take out a warrant against Kennedy on a capital charge of piracy. Transferred to Marshalsea Prison and finally cornered, Kennedy offered to turn King's Evidence on eight other pirates who had escaped with him from Argyllshire in exchange for a pardon. Only one of these men was arrested. He proved he was a forced man and was later released.

Kennedy was subsequently convicted of piracy at the Old Bailey and hanged at Execution Dock in July 1721. This ended a blood-soaked career that stretched back two decades, a rare achievement for a Blade of Fortune, whose average life expectancy was under 30.

CHAPTER 5

The Scottish Slavers & the Pirates

Ten days before Woodes Rogers set foot on New Providence in July 1718, the ship *Loyalty* of Port Glasgow weighed anchor from the Tail o' the Bank holding ground off Greenock. Under the command of Captain Mungo Graham, she was setting out on an extended 'triangular voyage' to Virginia via Liverpool, the Guinea Coast and Barbados. She was one of three Clyde vessels that are known to have been sent out in this despicable trade in human beings in the space of eighteen months.

Captain Graham received his final instructions from his somewhat naïve Glasgow owners, John Bogle, Richard Graham and William Anderson, to keep *the ship sufficiently with hogsheads and barrells and hope that during the course of the voyage you will exert the utmost dispatch and provide Cheap [the supercargo] with necessaries aboard and abed in the cabbin and use her civilly – keep a good watch over the negroes.*

Due, no doubt, to their inexperience, much time was wasted equipping the hull for its new purpose and getting there. For it was not until the following year that the *Loyalty* was on the Guinea Coast. Languishing in light airs off Cape Appollonia that May, she was attacked by the flotilla of Davis, Cocklyn and La Bouche who had resumed their joint cruise after burning Bance Island fort in the Sierra Leone River.

Captain Graham knew better than to offer resistance, as this would incur a good 'drubbing' at the hands of the boarders who came alongside. The pirates, led by 'Lord' Roger Hughes, spent the rest of the day looting the *Loyalty*'s cargo before stripping her of rigging and furniture. On their departure they forced the ship's cooper, John Daniels, and several other of the more skilled seamen of the twenty-man crew to go with them. The ship's surgeon, David Alexander, was, fortunately for him, allowed to remain behind. The presence of Dr Murray on Davis's *King James* probably saved him from years in captivity.

This was the second Scottish slaver they had ransacked within days on that part of the coast They had previously clambered onto Captain Aikenhead's vessel caught close inshore and took what they wanted before letting her go. What was the eventual fate of this vessel is not known, as she disappears from the records. It is likely that, after being left in a much-reduced state after the attack, she was lost to a slave insurrection on the coast or at sea while attempting the middle passage.

The *Loyalty* did eventually refit sufficiently to make it to Barbados with fifty-one enslaved Africans. She was back in Greenock by May 1720, after an absence of nearly two years. Her commander, Mungo Graham, had died in the interim and so she was brought home by the first mate. By this time the cooper, Daniels, had also reappeared at Greenock, having escaped from the pirates. By then the full chain of events of what happened, between the attack on the *Loyalty* off Cape Appollonia and the arrival of the pirate snow *Eagle* in Loch Craignish, had been pieced together by Campbell of Stonefield from the inmates of Inveraray Jail.

Shortly after the capture of the *Loyalty*, Davis on the *King James* parted company from La Bouche and Cocklyn after a drunken and acrimonious exchange of views. Off Cape Three Points he came up with a large Ostender, *Mark De Campo*, of thirty guns and ninety men heading for the East Indies. On board was the retiring Governor of Accra, his retinue and £15,000 in gold. Davis engaged her with a broadside, hoping to intimidate her captain into surrendering. To his surprise there followed a hot exchange that lasted for an hour before the Dutchman finally struck her flag.

Davis lost nine pirates to the Dutchman's shot, and so he forced those men found to be British in her crew. These additional hands were badly needed as he had decided to keep the Ostender, renaming her *Royal Rover*, to sail as his consort. Two of the forty-odd reluctant sailors taken that day were John Stewart and William Fenton, who were later among those hanged at Leith Sands.

The two pirate vessels sailed along the coast, aided by the strong easterly coastal current, to Anamaboe. This was one of the richest trading forts on the Guinea Coast. They arrived around midday on 5 June 1719 to find three English vessels, the galley *Princess*, the *Morrice* and the *Royal Hind*, at anchor awaiting slaves from Fort George.

It was a particularly fateful day, as among the forced men taken off the *Princess* was the third mate, the Welshman Bartholomew Roberts. Six of the Craignish pirates claimed that they were also taken then: John Eshwell and Thomas Rogers from the *Princess*; Dennis Toppen (or Topping) and William Fenton from the *Morrice*; and James Sail and John Gerrel from the *Royal Hind*.

Davis decided to abandon the *King James* as she rode to her anchors off the bar. After all his men and munitions had transferred to the *Royal Rover* (now mounting 32 cannons and 28 swivels), he set sail for Old Calabar. On arrival, he allowed his men shore leave for a drinking session and fraternisation with the local women.

This was when the *Loyalty*'s cooper, Daniels, made his escape and hid out until they had moved on. It was an impressive feat of survival, for a European straggler found by the local Efik traders would, as often as not, be sold back to his captors or bludgeoned to death. He was eventually taken on board a Dutch vessel heading back to Rotterdam, from where he made his way back to Greenock via Cork.

At Old Calabar the drunken orgy led to the inevitable murderous quarrel with the local inhabitants. Back at sea Davis pushed on round the Bight of Biafra looking for fresh opportunities. Anchoring off the Portuguese fort on the island of Principe, he decided to play his old trick of the 'visiting gentleman officer' again.

Introducing himself as an English naval captain chasing desperate pirates, he ingratiated himself with the Governor and his officers. A bungled attempt at molesting their womenfolk, however, almost tipped his hand. With suspicions already aroused, the tale of pirates, carried by an African boy who had swum ashore from the *Royal Rover*, was taken seriously. On Davis's next visit a carefully laid ambush was sprung. Davis fell fighting with a musket ball in his bowel, along with eight of his senior crew.

Fleeing out to sea, the 'Lords' on the *Royal Rover* called an election to appoint a new captain, in July 1719. This did not go the way some expected, as Roberts, who had only been forced aboard six weeks earlier, carried the day with the begrudging support of Lord Sympson.

His first act as captain was to avenge the death of Davis. Sailing back to Principe, the illiterate but fearless Walter Kennedy led the thirty-man assault party under the guns of the fort. The terrified defenders fled, leaving the pirates to burn the place after throwing the cannon into the sea. The town was then bombarded and two vessels set on fire before sufficient satisfaction was deemed to have been exacted from the Portuguese.

Off the neighbouring island of Anna Bona, with prizes getting scarcer and La Bouche and England still raiding back along the Guinea Coast, Roberts called for a vote – Brazil or the East Indies? The show of hands was for Brazil. The natives of Anno Bona obligingly provided the necessary provisions for the Atlantic passage. Fully stocked with *good eatables, caberitto ... hogs in abundance, yams and putato*, Roberts set the *Royal Rover* on a course for the small desolate volcanic islets of Fernando de Noronha, over 2,000 miles across the South Atlantic.

Several weeks later they entered the cove of the main island of this group. It was the dry season and they were hard put to find sufficient fresh water to replenish their butts. The island, being deserted and remote from the mainland, had no wildlife to hunt for food other than seabirds. It did, however, provide a safe haven for the *Royal Rover* to be careened and refitted.

Roberts' cruise of the Brazilian coast started badly. Sailing as far south as Bahia, he found that all worthwhile prizes were safely in harbour under the protection of forts. A fortnight passed before their luck changed. This was when they came upon two local fishermen in a small boat in the Bay of St Augustine. The Portuguese-speaking quartermaster Kennedy quizzed them and found out that a plate fleet had sailed just two days ago – information that *made Roberts very mad*.

The two Indians thought that another was soon due to sail from Pernambuco, the principal port further to the north. Roberts raced to intercept and came up with this fleet of forty-eight vessels just as they were forming-up prior to making way in convoy under the escort of two warships. Some way off the anchorage of Los Todos Santos, Roberts took a small straggling sloop without firing a shot. This provided him with the key to his strategy to cut out one of the great treasure ships without losing the element of surprise.

The sloop's captain was forced to point out the richest vessel in the *flotta*, the *Sacrada Familia* (40 guns, 150 men) – the Vice-Admiral's galleon. As the *Royal Rover* stood away under Kennedy's temporary command, Roberts sailed into the anchorage on the sloop filled with concealed fighting men. In doing so, he closed to within hailing distance of his selected prey without arousing suspicion. Indeed, the Portuguese master thought she was a dispatch boat and let her come alongside: *immediately Roberts clapped his four topsails aback, and fell on him, and lashed fast along side of his ship, and then he entered his Men, and in half an hour carried her.*

The stunned Portuguese Vice-Admiral and his crew were crammed on the sloop and cast off, leaving Roberts in full possession of the galleon as prize. On board was a fortune in gold coins consisting of 40,000 Portuguese moidores and 50,000 English guineas.

The capture had not gone unnoticed as neighbouring vessels let fly their top gallants and fired cannon to alert the two warships. These immediately slipped their anchors to give chase, but as the prisoner Richard Luntly later described, they were *as good as a cow after a hare*. Rogers easily made good his escape on the galleon, running north with the *Royal Rover* in close attendance.

Once clear of his pursuers, Roberts made for Devil's Island (Tortuga) off Guyana to consider his next move. There his crew indulged themselves in a two-week-long orgy while he consulted with his quartermaster Kennedy. The most recent news they had from the local governor was that the South Seas Company had hired a number of armed vessels to hunt down pirates found cruising in the Caribbean.

They decided therefore, that having hit the jackpot with the taking of the Portuguese galleon, it would be rash to risk capture by lingering too long in this sea area. Madagascar and the East Indies were to be their next hunting area. It was late in the year, so they decided to winter in the waters around Barbados before attempting to recross the Atlantic next spring. That agreed, they turned their minds to a more immediate problem, that of provisions. Their large pirate crew had, by now, got through or wasted most of what had been stowed on the *Royal Rover* at Anno Bona.

A solution to this problem seemed to be close at hand. On first entering the harbour at Tortuga, they had fallen in with a small New England sloop. This they took without a fight. Her grovelling captain sought to ingratiate himself with his captors by volunteering the information that he had only recently parted company with a large brig carrying victuals to the plantations. The sighting of sail out to sea, days later, triggered Roberts into making a snap decision. This was to leave the galleon and the *Royal Rover* at anchor under the charge of Kennedy, while he took forty men in the captured sloop to chase the provision ship.

According to Defoe, Roberts lost sight of the brig some thirty leagues to leeward of Devil's Island and gave up the chase. With the currents and wind against him he was unable to work his way back to his base. Languishing in light airs in an open sea, he was soon facing a water crisis. Leaving in such a great hurry, he had not had time to take on the extra supply needed by his large fighting crew. His solution to this problem was to dispatch the long-boat, which the sloop had been towing, to row back to fetch assistance from Kennedy. Days later the long-boat returned with the news that the *Royal Rover* – along with the treasure, the Portuguese galleon, Kennedy and the rest of his crew – had gone.

Luntly claimed, in his *Last Speech & Dying Words*, dictated in Edinburgh Castle vaults while he awaited execution, that he and the other accused had tried to seize the captured sloop the night before Roberts boarded her for the chase. Their intention was to escape before they were carted off to the East Indies and to turn themselves in to the nearest British Governor. This plan was thwarted when they were overheard by a Blade who reported them to Roberts and Kennedy. Immediately *all Hands were called up to know what they should do with us, some of them were for shooting us, others not, and so they consented to have us put away on a Desolate Place.* The sighting of the brig at first light saved them from this fate.

Some time during Roberts's eight-day absence, Kennedy was elected captain, despite the fact that he had no skills as a navigator or as a sailing master. He decided that the company should quit the business while they had a gold hoard to see them into a comfortable retirement. At this time, however, there were no more pardons to be had. Indeed, the local governors, following the example of Rogers and Spottiswoode, were summarily hanging all recidivist pirates found in American waters. Kennedy's plan was, therefore, to make for the remote part of the west coast of Ireland, as Captain Avery had done on his retirement two decades before.

To achieve this, the avenging Roberts would have to be thrown off their scent. At the same time a small anonymous vessel had to be found that would be suitable for entering an Irish bay without raising suspicion. Both aims required that the large and distinctive Portuguese galleon and the heavily armed *Royal Rover* (an ex-Dutch East Indiaman) were got rid of.

Kennedy's first step was to give away the Portuguese galleon to the obsequious master of the New England sloop, after transferring all the gold specie and dust to the *Royal Rover*. His second move presented itself off Jamaica in the last week of December 1719. This was when he came across his perfect retirement vessel – the 100-ton snow *Eagle* of New York. This four-year-old, two-decked vessel was laden with a cargo of victuals bound for Barbados. Kennedy's problem of feeding his pirate crew during the transatlantic crossing was thereby solved at a stroke.

The gold hoard was transferred to the *Eagle*, after which the *Royal Rover* was set on fire. Days later Roberts, pursuing them in his little sloop, found her drifting in the expanse of the Atlantic and burnt to the waterline. Kennedy and his treasure had vanished without a trace.

It was not all plain sailing for Kennedy on his way to Loch Craignish in Argyllshire. Early on in the five-week passage, his lack of seamanship almost sparked a mutiny among his men. At one stage, a number of them were for throwing him overboard but his prowess as a fighting man checked this impulse.

When he stopped a small unarmed trader off Barbados under the command of a Quaker, Captain Knot, bound for Virginia, eight of the most disgruntled jumped ship. They thought that they could bribe the pacifist captain to land them quietly along the coast of Virginia. They misjudged their man. For as soon as they had rowed ashore, and he was safely out of their clutches, he went straight to Governor Spottiswoode who had them rounded up and hanged in a matter of days.

The disappearance of the *Royal Rover* did not mean that the Scottish slavers on the Guinea Coast were now free from the threat of the New Providence pirates. In the same week that Kennedy burned her, the small brigantine *Hannover* of Port Glasgow weighed anchor off Greenock. She had on board sixty tons of assorted trade goods and was bound for the Guinea Coast. She was the third Clyde vessel to set sail for those parts in 1718 and 1719.

The capture and looting of the two preceding slavers by pirates was not, as yet, known to her Glasgow owners, Robert Bogle junior, Thomas Thomson, Samuel McCall, Arthur Tran and John Gray. They were, therefore, highly optimistic as to the success of this latest venture in which they had invested over a year in the planning. It was plainly an entirely new area of business for them as they had turned to the Scots network, at home and abroad, for guidance in all matters. By doing so they left behind the earliest and most complete record of a slaving venture.

Their key agent in London (the centre of the British slave trade) was the highly experienced and trusted Claud Johnston, previously a merchant of Edinburgh. He was directly responsible for the purchase of the core cargo of the essential Guinea goods – copper bars, pewter ware, ceramic beads, carpets, gunpowder, guns and swords – without which business could not be conducted. These trade goods had to be of the specific size and type demanded by the African traders.

He probably also arranged the acquisition of the small 60-ton *Hannover* from the South Sea Company and the retention of the services of her master, Garret Garrets, an American. Likewise, the recruitment of the 'Guinea surgeon', Alexander Horsburgh, in London, was almost certainly his handiwork, as the owners professed no knowledge of him prior to his appointment.

It was the Glasgow partners, however, who made the decision to bestow the additional key role of supercargo on Horsburgh for the outgoing voyage. No doubt impressed by his previous experience on the Guinea Coast, they empowered him – by a 'carte blanche' commission – to act on their behalf in all matters concerning the disposal and acquisition of cargo. Indeed, they ordered that should Garrets die in passage, Horsburgh was to assume the captaincy of the *Hannover*.

This trust, they later bitterly claimed, was betrayed and their interests wilfully abused. The result was an abysmal commercial failure for the promoters while Horsburgh profited – by his monthly salary and 'head money' as the ship's surgeon and by trading in slaves on his own account – at every turn. They seem to have been oblivious to the fact that the *Hannover* had led a charmed life during her voyage, as she had, unknown to all, narrowly missed being taken by pirates on a number of occasions during her voyage.

The full extent of this situation did not, of course, become apparent to the Glasgow promoters until the *Hannover* arrived back at Port Glasgow early in 1721. In her hold was the net result of a year's transatlantic trading: *not above twenty tons of sugar*. Absent was the supercargo responsible for this appalling return on their investment. In a letter delivered by Captain Garrets' hand, Horsburgh explained that he had taken the unilateral decision to send back his charge while he stayed on at the island of St Kitts to secure the next crop of sugar. In the interim he had drawn bills against their London account to pay himself his outstanding expenses, commissions and wages and that of the crew.

The Glasgow owners were incensed by his *fait accompli* and immediately set in motion the means to exact satisfaction. By the ruse of a placatory goodwill letter sent back with the *Hannover* they coaxed their erring supercargo out of his overseas bolt-hole. He arrived at Port Glasgow's quayside on 23 October 1721, along with his latest stockpile of sugar that amounted to a paltry six tons. Within sixteen hours of stepping ashore he was summarily arrested *like a criminal* by the owners' agents holding private *warrants to incarcerate at Random [issued by] inferior Judges [who] winked at such practises*.

He was immediately carted off to the Glasgow Tolbooth where he was imprisoned and refused bail: *he being a stranger to the place, such friends as he had [were] at a distance and ... they would not have been able to have satisfied the demands of such a clamorous Lybole*. Such was the serious nature of their charges and the legal precedents raised that the case was transferred to the High Court of Admiralty sitting at Edinburgh.

Horsburgh was moved to the Edinburgh Tolbooth where he lay for a further three months. During his imprisonment (in the depths of a Scottish winter, having spent the last year in the tropics) he fell dangerously ill. With the life of their quarry in the balance, his pursuers withdrew their opposition to bail. This was set at the enormous sum of £200 and was only found when two sympathetic Glasgow surgeons, Henry and John Marshall, rallied to the aid of a colleague, whereupon he was released to recover his health and prepare his case.

During his incarceration the owners and their lawyers had been busy scrutinising his *Tradeing Journall on the Coast of Guinea 1720*. This handwritten ledger had been forcibly taken from him at the time of his arrest, along with the cargo manifests and general correspondence, and later produced in court as the prime body of evidence as to his malpractice.

From such unique documentation the original business plan can readily be reconstructed. It was deceptively simple. Horsburgh was to supervise the loading of the 'Guinea' cargo that had been acquired in London and transferred (via Leith) to the owners' cellars in Port Glasgow over the past year. He was then instructed to make for Cork to receive any final consignment of trade goods forwarded by Claud Johnston from London, after which he was to sail directly to the Guinea Coast and there trade for slaves as only he knew best.

When 'fully slaved' he was to cross the Atlantic to Barbados where resident Glasgow-connected agents would advise him on market conditions on the principal 'Scots' sugar islands – St Kitts, Nevis and Antigua. Acting on this advice he was to make for the best option and there place himself under the direction of one of three Scottish planters named by the owners. The planter was to oversee the sale of the slaves and the acquisition of sugar for the return passage to Port Glasgow. The promoters fully expected to reap a sixfold return on their original stock of trade goods (£988) when this final cargo was sold to the 'Glasgow suggaries', in which they also held shares.

This plan, however, assumed expediency, given the perishable nature of the 'middle cargo', and a sense of duty to serve the owners' interest by the serving officers. These attributes were apparently missing from the outset. The *Hannover*'s stay at Cork was both lengthy and expensive. This Horsburgh blamed, in a letter to the owners, on his compassionate attempts to retrieve the second mate, William Kerr, *who had gone to Dublin with a whore* after a drinking spree. The owners were later to point out that this drunken orgy was the direct result of Horsburgh's foolish decision to allow Kerr an advance against his wages.

The *Hannover* sailed without the mate seven days later. In the interim it had loaded 200 locally supplied cows' horns, twenty gallons of smuggled French brandy and a further forty trade guns, to which were added a few more chests of Guinea goods (including old bed sheets) forwarded by Johnston from London. She sailed in the company of two London West Indiamen who offered protection from Barbary corsairs as far south as the 'western isles' (Madeira and the Canaries).

In early March 1720, just over two months after leaving the Clyde, she finally arrived on the Windward Coast of Africa. As the slaving fort on Bance Island was burnt out, Horsburgh exploited the inshore current to call in at a number of the smaller anchorages along the Ivory Coast during the next three weeks.

In this way he purchased two tons of rice and acquired twenty-one enslaved Africans in small consignments brought out by boat. He continued this strategy along the Gold Coast (5 April to 2 May) loading seventy-five chests of corn and increased his stock of onboard slaves to forty-three (one-third of the available berths). This was a poor result for two months' trading on this hostile coast during which the slaves had to be fed and kept in health.

It was also a highly dangerous gambit, as the risks of a slave insurrection and attack by pirates dramatically increased, the longer the vessel lingered inshore. These factors must have weighed on Horsburgh's mind, for he abandoned his search for slaves in the isolated inlets and proceeded directly to the Cross River townships that constituted Old Calabar. This port-of-call had been singled out by the owners in their scheming back in Glasgow as an area independent of the Royal Companies. There it was much easier for an 'interloping' Scottish slaver to deal in larger numbers of slaves with the local Efik traders – albeit at an exorbitant 'comey' (commission).

If Horsburgh had followed his owners' instructions and not wasted time at Cork or on visiting the creeks of the Gold Coast, he would have been at Old Calabar months earlier. He was blissfully unaware that, had he done so, the *Hannover* would have been in the clutches of either La Bouche or Edward England.

These two companies of pirates had separated to raid along the Guinea Coast ever since Roberts left Anno Bona for Brazil on the *Royal Rover*. Indeed, they had only just left Old Calabar for Madagascar and their rendezvous with Captain Macrae on the *Cassandra*, when the *Hannover* dropped anchor off the bar of the Cross River.

Not that the remainder of the *Hannover's* voyage was trouble-free, as a serious incident occurred on 18 May 1720, that put paid to any prospect of recouping lost time and profits. Four of the crew, led by the headstrong first mate, decided to *disobey express and repeated orders* and rowed ashore. They did so fully armed, as Horsburgh sarcastically recorded in his journal: *perhaps with a design to take the whole Continent of Africa*. On stepping onto the beach at Tom Shott's Point they were seized by the local Africans, who murdered one seaman on the spot and carried off the other three.

Horsburgh later claimed that, as they faced certain death if abandoned, he had no choice but to hire canoes to follow them upriver to negotiate a ransom from their captors. The latter he described as *men of no trade in Calabar, but I was obliged to comie them in order to get the white men again*. This complex business took two weeks and over £60 worth of prime cargo as 'comey' to King Ambro, five of his wives and ten retainers, before the suitably chastened mate and the two other seamen were released.

It was, therefore, late May before Horsburgh resumed his primary mission. This he evidently did with a sense of urgency for once. In a relatively short period of time, he traded over £800 of the owners' stock to acquire seventy-five slaves and 11,400 yams to feed his human cargo during the middle passage. When the 'fully slaved' *Hannover* finally cleared out of the Cross River, on 2 July, she had 134 enslaved Africans crammed under hatches, sixteen of whom had been purchased on Horsburgh's own account.

Illness and death followed the *Hannover* on *its unaccountable long passage* from Old Calabar, round the Bight of Biafra to the Portuguese island Anno Bona and finally out into the Atlantic. In the 'middle passage' she was beset by *contrary winds and calms*, finally reaching Barbados almost two months later. Yet again, her delayed arrival saved her from capture by a pirate company – this time that of Bartholomew Roberts.

After Kennedy had absconded with the *Royal Rover*, Roberts was left with a small sloop of ten guns and around forty men. This was a woefully inadequate force with which to hunt and survive as a pirate in Caribbean waters that were now regularly patrolled by commissioned armed cruisers. Indeed, while chasing Kennedy he was almost taken by one off Barbados. He only managed to escape after dumping his cannons and most of the cargo overboard. He had another narrow shave off Martinique that diverted his rage onto the inhabitants of these two islands.

With things too hot for his diminutive vessel, he sailed away to a safer sea area – Newfoundland. Arriving in the unsuspecting harbour of Trepassi he burned the fort and forayed amongst the fishing vessels. He kept a large French hull as his new flagship and renamed her the *Royal Fortune*.

Restored in firepower and men, he attempted to cross to Africa but was headed off by bad weather and only just made it back to the American seaboard before the last of the water on board gave out. So thwarted, he returned to the Caribbean in September 1720, in time for the arrival of the *Hannover*. Once there he unfurled his newest black flag, that of a pirate holding a cutlass and standing on two skulls. Underneath one foot were the letters 'ABH' (A Barbadian Head) and the under the other 'AMH' (A Martiniquean Head).

The *Hannover* arrived at Barbados on 31 October with a quarter of Horsburgh's cargo of 'sheep' already dead and flung overboard. This left him eighty-seven Africans to sell. Horsburgh made no mention of their suffering or condition in his journal when he paid himself 'head money' (12d. to the ship's surgeon for every live slave delivered in 'good condition' to the West Indies) against the owners' account. The only pointer to the causes of the death of the others was a deduction he made for the mate's outstanding wages (he had died in passage). This penalty, Horsburgh deemed, was warranted by his negligence when supervising the slaves on deck that allowed a female slave to jump overboard to her death while suffering from a bout of 'melancholia'. This term was then commonly used to cover any death brought about by acute depression induced by prolonged overcrowding below decks. The situation on board the *Hannover* must have been particularly terrible, as a number of his human cargo had been entombed on board for nearly nine months.

By the time the *Hannover* arrived at Barbados, Roberts had set up his base on the Windward Isle of St Lucia. From there he was kept busy for a time burning vessels in the harbours of the neighbouring French island of Martinique to avenge the previous actions of the island's governor.

Just over 100 miles away at Barbados, the *Hannover*'s cargo was quickly revived and 'polished' for sale. But, as Horsburgh informed his promoters (in a curt letter sent back by a London captain) the market had been lost by their delay. It was, therefore, a short stay during which he sold only three slaves at a low price of £21 each, as *the negroes are worth nothing here at present there has so many [been] sold here in the last two or three weeks and no money in the island.* Horsburgh promptly used what monies he received (including 147 ounces of silver) to pay himself and his crew their dues before sailing north to St Kitts.

Horsburgh arrived at this small Leeward Island on 1 November, and just missed Roberts's 'visit' on the *Royal Fortune* by a day. The island was recovering from the shock and still in the grip of military rule, as the Governor, Lieutenant-General Mathew, had the island's militia on full alert and the harbour blockaded after exchanging shots with Roberts.

The deluded Roberts blamed Mathew for the loss of the *Royal Rover* and the hanging of its pirate crew. He was plainly still completely unaware of the treachery of Kennedy and the true fate of his old flagship. It is clear from the threatening letter he sent in to Governor Mathew, while still hovering off the harbour mouth, that his rage had not diminished, even though almost a year had passed:

> *Royal Fortune, September the 27th, 1720*
> *Gentlemen,*
>
> *This comes expressly from me to let you know that had you come off as you ought to a done and drank a glass of wine with me and my Company I should not have harmed the least vessell in your harbour. Further it is not your Gunns you fired that affrighten me or hindred our coming ashore but the wind not proving to our expectation that hindred it. The Royal Rover you have already burnt and barbarously used some of our men but we have a new ship as good as her and for revenge you may assure yourselves here and hereafter not to expect anything from our hands but what belongs to a pirate. As further Gentleman, that poor fellow you have in prison at Sandy Point is entirely ignorant and what he hath he was gave him and so pray make conscience for once lett me begg you and use that man as an honest man and no a C[riminal] if we hear any you may expect not to have quarter to any of your island.*
>
> *Yours*
>
> *Barthw Roberts*

As it transpired, Roberts decided not to force a landing and sailed away, thereby allowing the *Hannover* to slip safely into the harbour a few days later.

Waiting to relieve Horsburgh of his role as supercargo was the resident Scottish planter, Colonel William McDowall. He was one of the three trusted advisers to the Glasgow circle that Horsburgh had been instructed to obey *as a cost experiment for the owners.* Under his instructions the remaining cargo of twenty-eight men, twenty-five women, eleven boys and four girls were sold in two lots.

It was, however, not a straightforward cash transaction with the other planters as there was very little sugar available on the island due to an *extrem drought.* McDowall was, therefore, obliged to sell the first lot (of sixty-two slaves) to 'two gentlemen' on the island at a best price of £24 for the prime men and £12 for the 'refused' (the sick and the weak). Getting rid of the final six slaves to the cash-strapped planters required a reduction in price (£22 for prime men) with payment set against the next crop of sugar, the harvesting of which had been postponed, due to the drought, until after Christmas.

By then the wily Horsburgh had sold off the residual cargo of Guinea goods and expended all new monies in his trust. He then played his trump card by ordering Garrets to take back the *Hannover* with what sugar was on the island, while he stayed on to await the new crop. Subsequently, the lightly laden brig left St Kitts for Port Glasgow with 20 tons and 101 quarters of sugar in her hold in mid-December.

By then two of the 'Lords' from Kennedy's crew of the *Eagle* had mounted the gibbet on Leith Sands. Around the same time Roberts was preparing to quit the Caribbean for African waters. This decision started the clock for his final showdown off Cape Lopez with Captain Ogle on HMS *Swallow*, which once and for all ended the menace of piracy in that region.

On 1 January 1724, three years after the arrest of the *Hannover's* supercargo, the action, Bogle *versus* Horsburgh, was finally called before Lord James Graham sitting on behalf of Charles, Duke of Queensferry and Dover, Vice-Admiral of Scotland.

The crux of the owners' grievance was that Horsburgh had been trading in the same commodity to the detriment of their interest. This, their lawyers argued, was contrary to the maritime Law of Nations as defined by European practice stretching back hundreds of years. In learned argument they reviewed the laws pertaining to the duties of a supercargo. Starting with the ancient laws of Rhodes, they progressed through the late medieval laws of the Île de Olernon, Wisburg and the Hanseatic League before concluding with the French Code of 1681. As a final measure they invoked Scots Law relating to the duties of a tutor (the supercargo) to safeguard the interests of an innocent tutee (the owners).

The pursuers insisted that the profit from the sale of Horsburgh's sixteen slaves was rightfully theirs. Failing that, he should be made to pay for the freight of his slaves to the West Indies and accept an 'average' number of dead in his quota. Indeed, they claimed that the high death rate amongst their slaves was a direct consequence of being tightly 'stowed' to make space for those belonging to him.

Horsburgh's pragmatic reply was that the owners must have been aware that he was carrying his own small trading stock before he left. Indeed, even if they had not, *nothing is more ordinary, all the world over, than for supercargoes to carry as many goods as their stock or credit will afford them, without acquainting the merchants*. He directly rejected their claims that he had mismanaged the care of the slaves or usurped his position *by which I had the opportunity of charging the dead ones to them*, all of whom, he claimed, had been differently 'marked' from his.

The owners were not so easily thwarted, and their petition was as multifaceted as it was tenacious. It catalogued other misdemeanours perpetrated by their supercargo (thirteen articles in all) against their interest. The main accusation was that he had no right to negotiate the 'extravagant' ransom for the captured mate and two crewmen at Old Calabar. The prime cargo he gave away for their release would have, they asserted, realised £350 worth of sugar in trade. Exorbitant personal expenses and highly suspect accountancy completed their list of grievances.

Horsburgh claimed that his open commission had empowered him to act in their best interest as he saw fit. This he had done in good faith, as *nobody would be a supercargo; it would be the hardest office that a man could undertake, [as] the least error might ruin him.* He also sought to turn the tables on the owners by pointing to their own incompetence and naivety. The copper bars (the main currency of the trade) they had bought in London were too short by the local standard used by the Efik African traders. The trade guns were badly rusted, having been left in damp cellars at Port Glasgow for over a year. Finally, they had bought a brig that was simply too small for the trade. With a burden of only sixty tons it could never deliver the economies of scale necessary to reach the profit margin anticipated by the owners.

The case lasted just over a year, during which many of Glasgow's merchant elite were called as expert witnesses for the pursuers. The most notable appearance was that of Richard Oswald of Stockwell Street and Scotstoun who was then the recognised authority on slave trading in Glasgow. Horsburgh was highly fortunate in that the two active members of the partnership – Thomas Thomson and Samuel McCall – had died and so could not testify as to the exact instructions given to him. Completing the wall of silence frustrating the pursuers was the disclaimer lodged by the ineffective Captain Garrets. In it he stated, no doubt to avoid criticism or liability, that he had never been consulted or made privy to any of the supercargo's decisions and had simply done as he was bidden throughout the voyage.

On 11 January 1725, Lord James Graham handed down his interlocutor on this complex case. Horsburgh was cleared of any liability for the losses incurred by his actions as supercargo – such was the open nature of his commission. He was, however, found liable for the freight of the slaves carried on his own account and was ordered to pay the owners £5 per slave.

This was not the end of this highly public and acrimonious affair. Two years later Horsburgh raised an action against the owners for his *false imprisonment* and *torture* at their hands. This petition was refused in January 1728.

All the major players in this drama survived the fallout of this dispute and prospered from the experience. The Bogle dynasty and their associates, having learned their lessons, moved on to make their fortune in direct trading from the Clyde to Virginia and Jamaica and back. The two prominent Scots planters on St Kitts (erstwhile garrison officers who came by their estates by marrying the widow Torie and her daughter Mary) also prospered by cutting out the Bristol middlemen and carrying their sugar directly to the Glasgow refineries in Clyde-owned vessels.

Colonel McDowall returned to Scotland in 1727 with sufficient wealth to restore Shawfield Mansion and purchase the Castle Semple estate near Lochwinnoch, Renfrewshire. Major James Milliken – McDowall's one-time adjutant – bought the neighbouring estate of Johnstone (which he renamed Milliken Park) and founded the great trading house of Alexander Houston & Co. of Glasgow. This firm crashed spectacularly at the end of the century while trying to corner the market for slaves in Jamaica.

Captain Garrets continued as to serve as a Guinea captain with different owners and eventually retired to America.

Horsburgh returned to sea and voyaged as far as China, from where he sent back samples of herbs and plants to his colleagues in Glasgow. He then settled in Glasgow and married the daughter of his saviour from the Tolbooth, the city's leading surgeon Henry Marshall. His subsequent election as a Fellow of the Royal College of Physicians and Surgeons of Glasgow underscored his full acceptance in local professional circles.

The cooper of the *Loyalty*, John Daniel, started his own legal action against the Bogles and their partners for his wages that they had stopped from the day he was captured by the pirates. This action he lost.

CHAPTER 6

John Gow:
the Orcadian Pirate

'The Pirate Gow' is the last major tale in the 1726 edition of Defoe's *General History of Pyrates*. Bundled in along with the story of the Irish murderer Roche, Gow is something of a misfit. Gow, while undoubtedly a brutal and bloody pirate, was not in the same league as the Brethren of the Coast who filled the rest of Defoe's book.

John Gow, alias John Smith, was a native of the village of Kerston, near Stromness in Orkney. At his trial at the Old Bailey for the murder of his former captain, Olivier Ferneau, and numerous acts of piracy, he steadfastly refused to enter a plea. He was plainly unaware that a charge of piracy, like that of witchcraft or treason, invoked a special dispensation to use judicial torture to *put the question* to the uncooperative.

The presiding magistrate, therefore, instructed the executioner to crush his thumbs with whipcord until he was forthcoming. This Gow endured several times before the cord broke. As he remained obdurate, the judge then ordered that he should be 'pressed' by great weights in the prescribed manner: *laid upon his back, with his body bare; that his arms be stretched forth with cord ... and that upon his body be laid as much iron and stone as he can bear and more. The first* day he shall have three morsels of barley bread, and the next he shall drink thrice the water in the next channel to the prison door but no spring and fountain water; and this shall be his punishment till he die. Gow was returned to Newgate Prison where he was shown what was entailed by a pressing. He immediately entered a plea of 'Not Guilty'.

It was, given the mountain of evidence and witnesses, a short trial. Gow, along with his first mate Williams and six of his crew, was found guilty and sentenced to hang at Execution Dock, Wapping on 11 June 1725. A seventh crewman, Alexander Robb, was executed a few days later. He had originally been sentenced to transportation but had caused so much trouble in his cell that this was changed to the death penalty.

The bodies of Gow and Williams received the customary encasement in chains and were left on public display hanging over the mud of Gallows Reach on the Thames until three tides washed over them, after which their bodies were given over to the 'anatomisers' (teaching surgeons and their students) for public dissection.

Gow's story had none of the epic proportions, exotic locations or dazzling treasure associated with the likes of Bartholomew Roberts. Gow earned his place in the *General History of Pyrates* by virtue of the number of throats he slit during his short but dramatic cruise off the north-west coast of Africa and the Iberian Peninsula.

What probably appealed to the 'carrion writer' in Defoe was the depths of depravity displayed during the first crime of mutiny, matched by the absurdity of his capture in his own home waters of Orkney. Defoe also had ready access to Gow whilst the latter was awaiting execution in Newgate Prison.

Gow had signed on to the *Caroline* galley (200 tons) at Amsterdam, pretty well intent on piracy. A previous attempt to raise a crew against their legal commander had failed miserably and he was lucky not to have been rumbled before. At Amsterdam, however, he found a kindred spirit and partner in crime, the Welshman James Williams. Williams almost certainly instigated the desertion of two Scots seamen from the *Margaret* of Burntisland, under Captain Andrew Watt, which was then anchored across from the *Caroline*.

They joined the *Caroline* just as she sailed for Santa Cruz in the Canaries. The galley was a well-armed vessel with twenty cannon and a crew of twenty-four. This was an adequate defence against the Barbary corsairs who swarmed out from their nests along the North African coast. She was also ideal for Gow's intended purpose – that of pirate cruiser.

During the two-month outward passage Gow and his co-conspirators worked relentlessly on the crew's sense of grievance; so much so that Captain Ferneau and his officers became aware of the mounting disaffection in the forecastle and were preparing their small arms against a possible mutiny.

Gow and his men, however, struck first during the first evening out from Santa Cruz en route for Genoa, on 3 November 1724. Three mutineers cornered and attacked the captain on the deck. He fought them off before Gow appeared and fired his pistol into his body. Bleeding profusely and still alive, Ferneau was thrown overboard.

With the whole crew now alerted to the mutiny, the mate and supercargo hid in the hold. Williams and Daniel McAuley (from Stornoway) soon tracked them down and cut their throats. Both victims, obligingly, managed to crawl on deck before expiring.

The ship's surgeon got as far as the stern before he was dispatched in a similar manner. With all the officers heaved over the side, the remaining crewmen were herded into the great cabin. There they were told that no harm would come to them if they followed orders and went about their duties.

At the age of 28, Gow realised his ambition when his eight fellow mutineers elected him their captain and the Black Flag was unfurled. The next few days were taken up with converting the galley, renamed the *Revenge*, to her new role, with additional cannon brought up from the hold.

Nine days after the mutiny Gow took his first prize, the *Delight* of Poole, bound for Cadiz from Newfoundland with a cargo of dried cod. Her captain, Thomas Wise, and his five crewmen were taken off the small sloop before she was ransacked and scuttled. Cruising towards the Straits of Gibraltar he fell in with his next victim, the snow *Sarah* of Glasgow, heading for Genoa with 'kitted' (boiled) salmon and salted herring under Captain John Somerville. Two of her crew, John Menzies and Alexander Robb, chose to turn pirate and joined Gow's crew. The *Sarah* was looted of her provisions and gear before being sunk.

Gow then chased a French vessel for three days before losing her in a fog bank. Running low in water, Gow set course for the Portuguese island of Madeira. Off Funchal he sent in an armed boat party to rifle what they could from any vessel they happened to find at anchor. This only succeeded in scaring off the local vessels and warned the local governor of the true nature of his visitors.

Gow's solution to his problem was to change his tactics and try again elsewhere. He subsequently, crossed the thirty-five-mile channel to the neighbouring island of Porto Santo. Running in under British colours he sent a polite note ashore asking the governor's permission to buy water and provisions. This was granted and the governor rowed out to pay his respects. Once on deck he was held captive until the water and provisions were forthcoming. The last items loaded were a cow and her calf and a coup full of chickens. The governor was then sent ashore with a present of beeswax.

So replenished, Gow set a course northwards to the coast of southern Portugal. Off Cape St Vincent, on 18 December, he took the American timber ship, the *Batchelor*, sailing under Captain Benjamin Cross. As before, the vessel was looted of its provisions. This time, however, Gow decided not to sink her but used her to rid himself of the captive crew of the *Delight*. Captain Wise and all but one of his men were duly put aboard and given a present of beeswax before being cast off. The cabin boy, William Oliver, was forcibly retained as Gow had the notion that he could be turned to piracy.

Nine days later, nearing Cape Finisterre and close inshore he struck again. She was a French vessel, the *Lewis Joseph*, heading north from Cadiz with a cargo of wine and fruit under Captain William Mens. After she was looted Captains Somerville and Cross were dumped on her along with a number of their crewmen and the now customary present of beeswax. Once out of sight of Gow, they altered course and headed for Scotland.

Twelve leagues off Cape Finisterre, the *Revenge* came up with a large and well-armed Frenchman that Gow refused to engage. The mate Williams was incandescent with rage at his cowardice. At the height of his tirade he drew his pistol and snapped it against Gow's head. It failed to fire. At this, two other pirates came to Gow's defence and discharged their pistols at Williams, wounding him in the arm and belly. With some difficulty he was eventually overpowered and clamped in irons below.

Three days after this incident, some thirty leagues off Vigo, Gow stopped the *Triumvirate* of Bristol, on her way south with a cargo of fish under Captain Joel Davis. She was extensively looted and her long-boat taken before Gow ordered the remaining members of the *Sarah* to board her. Two forced crewmen from the *Caroline* at the time of the mutiny pleaded with Gow to let them go too, but he refused, claiming their skills were too valuable to lose.

The wounded Williams was, however, expendable and so he was dragged up and heaved onto the *Triumvirate*. Gow requested that Captain Davis turn him over to a British naval commander to be hanged as a pirate at the first opportunity. This Davis duly did as HMS *Argyle* was in Lisbon en route for Sheerness at the time of his arrival.

Gow's two-month cruise as a pirate had yielded little in the way of wealth other than a collection of sea captains' gold and silver watches. He had intended to cross to the Caribbean and emulate the Brethren who had taken fortunes in plate from the Spanish. His lack of provisions put paid to that idea. Instead, he decided to retire with what he had before the net closed around him. And so he quit Iberian waters and sailed back to Orkney and his hometown of Stromness. During the voyage the galley's name was changed again, to the more peaceful sounding *George*.

Foolishly, Gow took with him a crew of thirty men, most of whom were now lukewarm about their career as pirates and anxious to desert. Gow, nevertheless, rehearsed them in their cover story. This was that they were driven into Stromness by adverse weather while going 'north-about' round Scotland from Cadiz heading for Stockholm. To strengthen their resolve and silence the waverers, he devised a set of standing orders that were to be followed to the letter:

1. *That every man shall obey his commander in all respects as if the ship were his own, and be under monthly pay.*

2. *That no man shall give or dispose of the ship's provisions. Whereby may be given reason of suspicion that everyone hath not an equal share.*

3. *That no man shall open or declare to any person what we are or what design we are upon; the offender shall be punish'd with death on the spot.*

4. *That no man shall go ashore till the ship is off the ground and in readiness to put to sea.*

5. *That every man shall keep his watch night and day, and precisely at the hour of eight, leave off gambling and drinking, everyone repair to their respective stations.*

6. *Whoever offends shall be punish'd with death; or otherwise as we shall find proper for our purpose.*

This was nailed to the mainmast and was still there at the time of their capture on the Calf islet in the Sound of Eday.

The change of events and coincidences that led to his downfall intrigued Defoe as much as his acts of *Murther and Piracy*. Indeed, in his one-shilling *An Account of ... John Gow* (published under his own name by Applebee), the subtitle proclaims: *A Relation of all the horrid MURTHERS they committed in cold blood AS ALSO their being taken at the Islands of Orkney and sent up Prisoners to London.*

Gow's motives for returning to Stromness were a mixture of necessity – the galley badly needed her sides cleaned and required to be provisioned – and a misplaced sense of security. He brought the *George* in to the roadstead in mid-January 1725 and received a warm welcome from the inhabitants. Here was a local son who had obviously done well for himself and was now captain of a large ship. His crew behaved themselves well enough while ashore and traded their cargo of beeswax and copper for wine and brandy in a open-handed way. In between times, they were kept busy cleaning a side of the *George* at low tide. No one ashore asked too many questions, as this was an area steeped in smuggling.

Unfortunately for Gow, the *Margaret* of Burntisland came to anchor close by and her captain recognised the *Caroline* – despite the repainting of her stern and change of name. Captain Watt made it his business to row over and demanded to know the whereabouts of the two deserters from his ship. Gow gave him short shrift, first denying their presence on board and then refusing to turn them over to him.

All might have gone well for Gow had he cleared out immediately, but he still had the other side of the hull to clean. This delay was to be his downfall for, unknown to him, Watt met up with one of his deserters, Harry Jamieson, while ashore. Jamieson gave Watt a full account of the events since he had jumped ship at Amsterdam. Watt realised that they were both in mortal danger. Gow was not only a cold-blooded murderer, but also the master of the eighteen cannon on the *George*. He could inflict a terrible act of reprisal on the *Margaret*, should Watt make public Jamieson's information. Watt, therefore, advised the young seaman to get away while he could. The captain had already decided to tell the authorities about the pirates in their town only when he was about to make sail.

Jamieson went straight back on board the *George* to avoid suspicion. He must, however, have told a number of his fellow crewmen what Watt intended to do, for on the evening the

Margaret sailed (1 February) ten men escaped from the *George* on the long-boat.

These men spent that night on a small island in Scapa Flow before they rowed across the Pentland Firth to Caithness on the Scottish mainland. There they tried to turn themselves in to the local Justice of the Peace. He was not prepared to deal with them and sent them on their way after feeding them. At Fortrose they sold some of their clothes for food before breaking up – five heading for Glasgow, four to Aberdeen and one to his hometown of Banff.

By now Gow's plan to slip away quietly was falling apart. As he made his final preparations to leave, one of his men, Robert Read, a native of Cromarty, deserted whilst ashore. Running inland, he told a farmer his tale and was given a horse to ride the twelve miles to Kirkwall to inform the authorities. In the meantime the farmer raised the alarm in the local area.

It was a timely warning, for Gow had decided to resort to a pirate press-gang to make good his losses in manpower. Two men were taken off a small vessel in the harbour, while another two were grabbed off a street in Stromness. Three others volunteered, not knowing the nature of the voyage. Gow even managed to recruit his 14-year-old nephew. As he was ashore doing so, two more crewmen deserted: William Oliver, the cabin boy from the *Delight*, and the informer Harry Jamieson, who escaped dressed as a woman.

On 10 February Gow decided to make sail even though the *George* had still only been cleaned on one side. His last act before departing was to send an armed shore party to Graemsay Island, two miles to the south. Led by the boatswain, James Belbin, their mission was to loot the great house of Robert Honeyman of Graemsay, the High Sheriff of Orkney.

When they arrived they found the master of the house absent. He had been called away to Kirkwall to deal with Read's report of pirates. So it was left to his formidable womenfolk to confront the pirates when they broke in. Honeyman's daughter escaped through an upper window with the charter chest. Her mother hid most of the money kept in the house in the folds of her dress. The pirates came away with only seven pounds in cash and a few silver spoons. They did, however, abduct the resident piper, Edward Gunn, and two servant girls.

These women were, after some dalliance, later put ashore on Cava Island in Scapa Flow with sufficient gifts to enable them to find husbands. Defoe played this incident for all it was worth, claiming that they were actually taken from Cava and wrenched from the pleading arms of their mother and that they were terribly abused during their short captivity on board the *George*.

By then news of the raid on Graemsay's house had reached Kirkwall, where frantic preparations were being made to repel the anticipated pirate attack. Sheriff Honeyman chaired a meeting of local magistrates and town councillors to deal with the emergency. They ordered:

> *twenty-four men, furnished with good and sufficient arms, to keep guard at the Tollbooth ... and appoint that the town's guns and haill other armes belonging to the inhabitants to be made ready for service, and lykeways appoint the great guns belonging to the burgh, now in the church, be carried down to the fort at the shoarre ... to issue forth a proclamation advertising the haill inhabitants ... by tuck of drum to rendezvous before the Tollbooth this afternoon.*

However, Gow had another easier target in mind. This was Carrick House near the hamlet of Calfsound on the island of Eday. This property was owned by an old acquaintance, James Fea of Clestrain. To achieve the element of surprise, while avoiding any custom cutters or naval sloops that might be waiting for him off Kirkwall, he sailed due north from Stromness and rounded Papa Westray into the North Sound.

On his final approach to the inner Sound of Eday, Gow made the greatest mistake of his life as he entrusted the helm and pilotage to one of his new and reluctant men, Robert Porringer of Westray. While going about at the entrance Porringer 'missed stays'. The galley immediately lost headway and fell back under the influence of the strong rip tide. Swept onto the nearby Calf of Eday, she grounded on the islet.

This mistake could have been rectified easily and the galley got off undamaged by 'kedging'. This required the ship's anchor and cable to be rowed out to deep water and dropped, after which the crew at the capstan could haul the galley up to the anchor, pulling the *George* off the ground. The weight of the great anchor, however, was such as could only be supported by a large long-boat. The small sailing dinghy that Gow had on deck was wholly inadequate and would have sunk under the weight. Unfortunately for Gow, at that moment his long-boat, taken from the *Triumvirate*, was lying on the hard standing at Thurso, over fifty miles away. There was, though, one suitable vessel very close at hand, a two-ton salt boat that belonged to his intended victim, James Fea.

Fea was watching from the shore of the main island when the *George* grounded. It was three days since the raid on Graemsay's house and the news had already reached this remote part of the islands. He knew that Gow would sooner or later have to send ashore for assistance. This happened late in the morning when an unarmed shore party rowed over in the dinghy. Fea was waiting, musket in hand, and refused to let them land. Instead, he gave them a letter he had prepared. It was addressed to his one-time schoolfriend, John Gow, and made it clear that he was aware of how things stood: *All the inhabitants of this place have fled to the hills because of the bad reports that your enemies have reported of you thro this countrey which I hope is groundless.*

From the brief encounter with his shore party, the astute Fea had deduced Gow's predicament. He ordered his men to have all the boats on the island hidden along with their sails. He also had a lower plank in his salt boat staved in so as to make her unseaworthy. Finally, he sent a dispatch to Kirkwall to seek assistance with the pirates.

That afternoon Gow sent back a five-man shore party led by the boatswain. This time they came heavily armed and with instructions to force the local inhabitants to co-operate. As there were very few firearms on the island with which to repel them, Fea feigned compliance and bid them join him in a drink at a nearby hostelry. This offer was readily accepted.

As proceedings got more and more convivial, Fea invited the lecherous boatswain to visit his house to pay his respects to his good wife. This he accepted, leaving the other four pirates to their whisky. Fea had men waiting in ambush along the road and Belbin was taken by surprise and, after a violent struggle, tied up. By the time Fea returned to the inn with his men, the four pirates were so drunk that they offered little resistance to their captors. All five were securely tied up and marched away to the other side of the island and out of reach of Gow.

In this incident, Gow had lost five of his willing Blades and the dinghy, as well as arming Fea's men with their captured firearms. His situation was now desperate and the following day he tried to sail the *George* off on the high tide. One of the forced men deliberately cut the anchor cable at the critical moment. Without an anchor to check her, the galley was driven hard up on the rocks at Calf Island at the top of the tide.

Gow was now stranded, with no hope of escape without Fea's help. He sent a pitiful letter by a messenger who walked across the islet waving a white flag as a signal to be picked up. In it he tried to move Fea with a mixture of bribery and suicidal threats: *If you'll grant me assistance I hereby oblidge myself to pay you the value of one thousand pounds sterling; [for] if it be my misfortune to be shipwrecked, the Government siezes all; and I'll take care they shall be nothing the better – only the guns; for I'm resolved to set fire to all and all of us perish together.*

There then followed a flurry of correspondence and parleys via a go-between, during which Gow upbraided Fea for not helping him as a friend, threatening to burn the galley and its cargo and then cast himself into the sea. In the end Fea lost patience and told Gow to give himself up before the navy arrived.

This stand-off would have continued much longer, had not the go-between, Scollay, disobeyed Fea's direct order and gone on board the *George*. Fearing that he was being held hostage, Fea led a second boat party with seven armed men over to Calf Island. After much discussion Scollay was escorted to the shoreline by Gow and the last two mutineers remaining at liberty, under a white flag of truce. Face-to-face with Gow at last, Fea seized the opportunity to make all three prisoners after a brief scuffle.

Those remaining on board were now leaderless and easily duped into coming ashore. This was done by a letter from Fea that promised them a boat on which to escape, but only if they gave over the *George* and its cargo. Before walking over to the rendezvous point, the last of the pirates broke open the ship's chest and they filled their pockets with what they could carry. By evening they had all been ferried across to Eday where they were, to their great chagrin, put in irons.

From there Gow and his crew were shipped over to Fea's main residence on the neighbouring isle of Shapinsay, to await the arrival of the agents of law and order. In the interim, Fea had Scollay organise the refloating of the *George* while his clerk set about cataloguing her cargo and contents as his prize.

On 26 February, nine days after the capture of Gow, the sloop-of-war, HMS *Weazell*, dropped anchor in Linga Sound. Her captain immediately dispatched his long-boat to take possession of the *George* as his prize. Fea was outraged but, as he could do little about it, he gracefully volunteered the use of his men in her salvage.

By the time they had the *George* refloated, on 5 March, the sixth-rater HMS *Greyhound* had arrived to take the prisoners to London for trial. Already on board were two of the men who escaped on the long-boat and had since been picked up in Aberdeen.

The authorities in Edinburgh and London had been aware of Gow's activities and general whereabouts even before the raid on Graemsay's house. Four days earlier, the released Captains Somerville and Cross had put into Stranraer on Loch Ryan on the *Lewis Joseph* and given their account to the local Customs Officers. This report was immediately relayed to their Commissioners in Edinburgh and London. Three days later Captain Andrew Watt, master of the *Margaret* of Burntisland, made his statement to officials as to what he knew about the fate of the officers of the *Caroline* galley.

By then HMS *Argyle* had already docked at Sheerness with the mate Williams as prisoner. It was the imprisonment of Williams in London and the availability of witnesses to the murders that gave the High Court of Admiralty sitting at the Old Bailey the jurisdiction to try the whole crew for crimes committed on the high seas.

Gow and thirty-one of his men left Orkney on 9 March as prisoners on board HMS *Greyhound*. James Fea also travelled with them as a passenger. His interest was the *George*, which sailed as part of the convoy under escort of HMS *Weazell*. They all arrived in the Thames together and the prisoners were marched off to Marshalsea Prison, Southwark on 30 March. After a preliminary hearing twenty-four were committed for trial and moved to Newgate Prison. In the interim, five of the forced men had been pardoned so as to give evidence for the prosecution.

After the trial and executions the legal wrangling over the prize vessels continued. The French owners of the *Lewis Joseph* could not be found at first and so advertisements had to be taken out in the London papers. Fea had an outstanding salvage claim on the *George* that the Admiralty had to square with that of the captain of HMS *Weazell*. To resolve all issues Fea was awarded £300 in salvage money, £1,000 for his astute and courageous capture of the pirates and a further £400 from the grateful marine insurers of London.

Back in Orkney, Fea's new-found wealth was the subject of much malicious gossip. As a well-known and barely concealed Jacobite, it did not take much for the local population to vilify him as an unscrupulous man who had come by his blood money by tricking men whilst under the white flag of truce. The insults were such that he spent much of his money and time in legal actions trying to clear his name. He was later to pay dearly for his allegiance to the Stuarts in exile. For his open support for Bonnie Prince Charlie, Butcher Cumberland's troops burned his house on Shapinsay.

Gow's legacy to Orcadian folklore includes the tale of his former sweetheart, Helen Gordon, who reputedly travelled to London intent on releasing herself from her promise to marry him. She had 'pledged her troth' years before by touching his hand through the hole of the Odin Stone, an ancient monolith that stood at Stenness. She arrived too late to speak with him as he had already been executed. So she touched his lifeless hand as he hung in chains on Gallows Reach to escape a visitation by his ghost.

1. Henry Avery (Every)

2. Edward England

3. Howell Davis

4. Bart Roberts

5. Captain James Macrae, Governor of Madras, with diamond tie pin (in a private collection)

6. Elizabeth, Dowager Countess Glencairn (National Galleries of Scotland)

7. James, 14th Earl Glencairn and friend of Burns (in a private collection)

8. Sir John Drummond of Quarrell, MP and Director of HEIC (in a private Scottish collection)

9. Macrae's Mausoleum, Monkton, Ayrshire (ESME Collection)

10. Lord Archibald Hamilton, Governor of Jamaica
(in the collection of Lennoxlove House, Haddington)

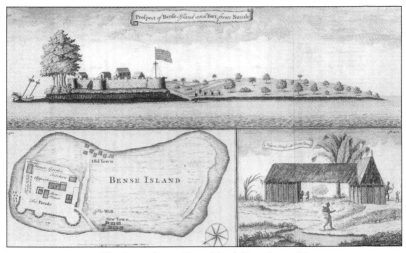

11. The slaving fort on Bance Island, Sierra Leone River
(ESME Collection)

12. Robert Louis Stevenson
(ESME Collection)

13. Flint's Treasure Map
(ESME Collection)

14. Greenock 1768

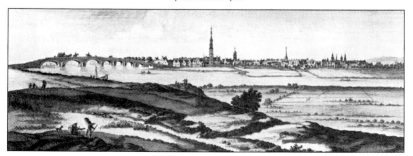

15. Glasgow 1693

16. Barbados

17. Sir James Graham,
Judge to the High Court of
Admiralty of Scotland
(in a private collection)

18. Robert Dundas of Arniston, Procurator
to the High Court of Admiralty of Scotland
(in the collection of the
Dundas-Bekker family, Arniston)

19. Heart of Midlothian – the Old Tolbooth of Edinburgh
(ESME Collection)

THE LAST

SPEECH

And Dying Words, of *John Clark*, condemned for Piracy, and executed at *Leith, December* 14, 1720.

I Confeſs that I was upon the Iſland of *Providence* when Governor *Rogers* came with the King's Pardon to the Pirates that were there; and that I was one of thoſe who was a pirating before I came into the *Buck-Sloop*: And it is no leſs true, that when we came out with the *Buck*, we intended to carry on a lawful Trade, but were prevented by the Inſurrection of the old Offenders, who took the Sloop away from theſe that came from *England* in it, of whom *Roger Hughes* was one. It is a great Trouble to me to think of the Suffering of this *Man* and others that are condemned to die. For alas I was at the Taking of them out of their reſpective Ships, and forcing them, much againſt their Wills, to go alongſt with us in a very wicked Courſe of Life. I go out of this World with a heavy Heart, when I think how innocently theſe Poor Men muſt ſuffer. If all thoſe who are taken by Pirates are ſentenced to die, a great many of the King's good Subjects will ſuffer unjuſtly.

I cannot go out of this World with any Peace of Mind without declaring publickly, that I think they are much wronged and unjuſtly condemned. Sentence might very juſtly have paſſed on the Doctor and me, for he and I were long engaged in theſe wicked Courſes. But as for theſe poor Men they were taken by us and others from their honeſt Way of getting Bread, and never did any of theſe Things they were accuſed of, but as they were forced to the Working of the Ship, which if they had refuſed they would have been ſhot to Death that Moment. It is no Wonder then that they complied ſo far; for it is natural for us to ſhun immediate Death, and to preſerve our Lives as long as we can. As I am a dying Man, I have told you nothing but the Truth of them.

Further I reckon I am bound in Conſcience to inform you, that thoſe poor Men who are now condemn'd, ſeveral Times, with the Hazard of their Lives, endeavoured to make their Eſcape from us; and I declare, on the Word of a dying Man, that I am perſuaded, That if Captain *Roberts* had met with them, they would all either have died by his Hand, or at leaſt been let a Shore on ſome deſolate Iſland.

Jt

20. John Clark's Dying Speech
(National Library of Scotland)

21. Pressing a pirate
(ESME Collection)

22. Pirates torturing a prisoner
(ESME Collection)

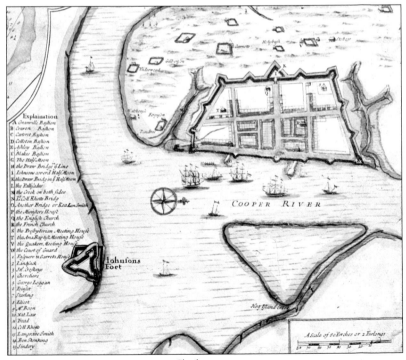

23. Charleston c.1700
(ESME Collection)

24. The hanging of Stede Bonnet
(ESME Collection)

25. View of South-east London
(ESME Collection)

26. Daniel Defoe
(ESME Collection)

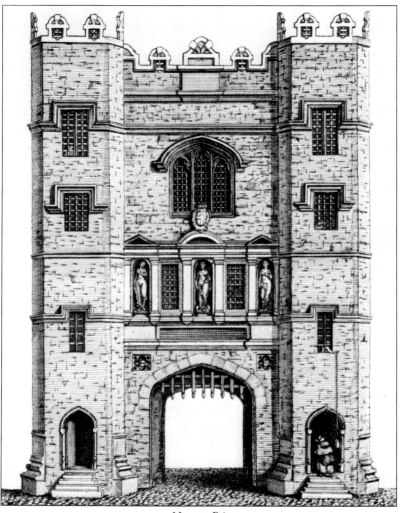

27. Newgate Prison
(ESME Collection)

28. *Gang-I- Sawai* from an Indian drawing (ESME Collection)

29. Kidd's execution
(ESME Collection)

30. Captain William Dampier
(ESME Collection)

31. Arms of the Company of Scotland
(ESME Collection)

32. Johanna Island, Comoros Islands c.1700
(ESME Collection)

33. Howell Davis – a Victorian view
(ESME Collection)

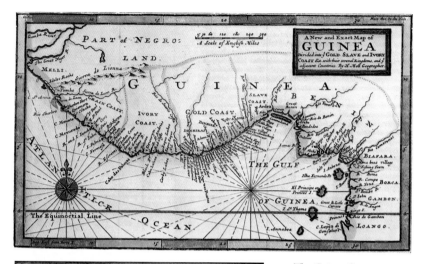

34. The Guinea Coast, 1740
(ESME Collection)

35. The Mogul Emperor
Aurungzeeb
(ESME Collection)

36. Madagascar c.1700
(ESME Collection)

37. Stornoway c.1800
(National Galleries of Scotland)

CHAPTER 7

The Scots &
the Pirate Crews

The exact number of men and women who went 'a-pirating' during the 'Golden Age' (the thirty years after 1694) will never be known. At the height of their activity in the Caribbean, when Woodes Rogers arrived to reform or evict the Brethren of the Coast from New Providence in 1718, there may have been as many as 2,400 on that one island.

Some eight years later, after this tidal wave of terror had run its course across half the globe, the numbers sailing under the Black Flag had irreversibly slumped to around 400. Most of them were holed up on the island of Madagascar in the Indian Ocean. During the intervening eight years, about the same number had met their end swinging from the gallows or the yardarm.

The 'high period' lasted only ten years. It started with the Lord Archibald Hamilton's treasure hunters departing for New Providence in 1716 and ended with the hanging of the last of the Brethren, William Fly, in Boston in 1726. This intense and spectacular period in maritime history has captured the public's imagination ever since.

Defoe's *General History of Pyrates* (written under his pseudonym of Captain Charles Johnson) is by far the greatest source to have survived from the period. The first edition (1724), relating bloodthirsty tales replete with details of pillage, rape and murder, was an immediate best-seller. It focused, understandably, on the dare-devil deeds of a handful of the most ruthless and bloody pirate captains. The Scots included in his rogues' gallery are William Kidd of Dundee and John Gow of Orkney.

Of the lives of the rank-and-file crew members, however, very little is known. Indeed, most were careful to nurture the cover of anonymity behind which they intended to slip back into peaceful society with their ill-gotten loot. The few names that were recorded were those unfortunate enough to have been caught and interrogated by officials (usually clergymen or surgeons) prior to being hanged. The great pirate historian of modern times, Philip Gosse, gleaned these names, along with those mentioned in the *Calendars of Newgate Prison*, and added them to Defoe's principal characters. The outcome was his *The Pirates' Who's Who*, first published in 1924. From this representative sample it would appear certain that the Celts (Welsh, Irish and Scots) contributed a disproportionately high number of villains, relative to the size of their seafaring populations.

With many pirate companies disbanding to take the pardon and individual pirates retiring with their loot without being caught, it is very rare to find piracy trials of large crews. Of the handful from the 'high period', the first was that of 'Major' Stede Bonnet and his thirty-one crew tried in Charleston in 1718.

Bonnet was a well-off Barbadian gentleman planter who seems to have been drawn into piracy by the spirit of high adventure the year before. He bought his own vessel, the *Revenge*, intending to be a legitimate privateer against the Spanish and join those plundering the wrecks of the Spanish plate *flotta*. Events, however, quickly carried him over that fine line that separates privateering from piracy.

He made a pretty poor pirate captain by all accounts. Defoe described him as *ill qualified for the business, as not understanding maritime matters*. He was, in fact, an ex-infantry officer whose attempts at imposing strict military discipline on his ruffian crew backfired. Indeed, most deserted to Edward 'Blackbeard' Teach on the *Queen Anne's Revenge* when the two captains met off the coast of Virginia in August 1717. They cruised together for nearly a year during which time Bonnet was humiliated at every turn and finally cheated out of his share of the booty. Bonnet took 'the pardon' the following spring and later obtained a privateering commission to cruise against the Spanish in the Caribbean from Charles Eden, the easily bribed Governor of Carolina.

On clearing out of Bath Town, however, he changed the name of his sloop to *Royal James*, and his own name to Captain Thomas, before reverting to piracy against local vessels. He was finally cornered and captured in the Cape Fear River of North Carolina in late September by two armed sloops. Their commander, William Rhett, had been searching for Charles Vane when the Governor of Charleston received the news of Bonnet's presence.

At Charleston, his crew of thirty-three men were tried for piracy and thirty were found guilty. Fortunately for posterity, the court recorded not only their names but also their last place of residence. Five gave a Scottish domicile: Neal Paterson, William Scot and William Eady were noted as 'late of Aberdeen'; while George Rose and George Dunkin said that they were from 'Glascow'. They were all found guilty and publicly executed on 8 November 1718 at White Point, Charleston and buried in the marsh below the high-water mark.

Bonnet and his first mate, David Harriot, were not with them as they had managed to escape a few days before the trial. After bribing their guards, they had stolen a small boat and sailed out to sea from Charleston, only to be blown back by bad weather. While sheltering on Sullivan's Island, Rhett tracked them down. The mate was shot dead and Bonnet was recaptured. His luck having finally run out, he was found guilty and sentenced to death. He pleaded for his life by offering, if pardoned, to render himself incapable of turning pirate again, by having his arms and legs amputated.

How Scotsmen came to be sailing with the Barbadian Bonnet on his 10-gun sloop was hinted at in the trial papers. They all claimed that they had been marooned before being rescued by Bonnet. They admitted that they had since participated in piratical actions but only because of the dire lack of provisions on board the *Revenge* (later *Royal James*).

This rather novel line of defence may have been based on fact. Two Scottish ships were among the twelve logwood traders caught and burned in the Bay of Campechy in 1716 by a Spanish taskforce. This was a reprisal for the attacks on the salvage ships working over the sunken wrecks of the plate fleet. At the time of the attack, the Spanish were content to burn the vessels of the interlopers, leaving their crews marooned.

That they did not plead that they were forced men, the time-honoured defence of all notorious pirates, is significant. The most likely explanation is that they had all chosen to 'turn' pirate and sign Articles when their Scottish merchantmen were captured. Bonnet is known to have looted the *Anne* of Glasgow (under

Captain Montgomery) for clothing, ammunition and provisions at the very start of his last pirate cruise. Some months later he boarded and ransacked three more Glasgow-bound tobacco traders off the Capes of Virginia. Likewise, the Aberdeen contingent may well have deserted from the captured *Young* of Leith.

The largest group of pirates ever tried were the crews of Bartholomew 'Black Bart' Robertss's squadron, comprising the *Royal Fortune*, the *Great Ranger* and the *Little Ranger*. They were the survivors of the fierce sea battle with Captain Chaloner Ogle on HMS *Swallow* in March 1722 that ended the reign of the Black Flag terror in African waters. Such was the nation's relief, that Ogle was given a knighthood. He is the only naval officer ever to have received this honour solely for capturing pirates.

At their trial at Cape Coast Castle, all of the 169 charged with piracy pleaded 'not guilty' on the grounds that they were forced men. Seventy-four had their plea accepted and were acquitted, while the rest were tried and found guilty. Of the latter, seventeen were sentenced to be transported in chains to Marshalsea Prison in London (eight died on the way), twenty were given as slaves to the Royal Africa Company to labour in their gold mines for the rest of their days, and fifty-three were hanged outside the gates of Cape Coast Castle.

As at Leith the year before, the first batch to march to the gallows outside the castle gates were those identified as members of the 'House of Lords'. These were the aristocrats of piracy by virtue of being members of the original New Providence Brethren. The *Swallow*'s surgeon, Mr Atkins, was in close attendance to ascertain their age and birthplace as they filed past.

Leading this grisly procession was the 36-year-old 'Lord' John Sympson, originally from North Berwick in East Lothian.

He had aided and abetted Howell Davis when he seized the *Buck*. Later, when Davis was killed in an ambush he had thought to challenge Roberts for the vacant position of captain. Measuring up his opponent, he thought better of it and threw his lot in with the Welshman. For that he was made quartermaster after 'Lord' Thomas Antis absconded with the appropriately named prize – the *Good Fortune*, taking a large share of the accumulated booty with him. It was, therefore, Sympson who was left to rally the crew of the *Royal Fortune* after Roberts was killed by a grapeshot ball that gashed his windpipe as he stood on his quarterdeck.

On his way to the gallows, Sympson displayed the fatalistic swagger expected of a pirate 'Lord' until he passed a woman in the crowd whom he recognised. On recovering his composure he arrogantly scoffed out loud, *I have lain with that Bitch three times, and now she has come to see me hanged.* The unfortunate subject of his outburst was Elizabeth Trengrove. She had been a passenger on the Royal Africa Company ship *Onslow* when taken by Roberts eight months previously. Sympson had, no doubt, exploited his position as quartermaster to appoint himself her guard. This had given him the opportunity to repeatedly abuse her, despite Roberts's Article concerning women on board.

She had finally been allowed to depart on one of the two small prizes that Roberts gave to the evicted crew of the *Onslow* when he took that vessel over as his last flagship, renaming her *Royal Fortune*. One of those prizes headed for Fort James in the Gambia River whilst the other, carrying Sympson's victim, made straight for Cape Coast Castle. She arrived in ample time to have the dubious satisfaction of witnessing his trial and execution.

She might have counted herself fortunate had she known the fate of the woman taken by Antis in the Caribbean at around the same time. That lady was a passenger on the Scottish vessel *Irwin*, under Captain Ross, carrying 600 barrels of beef from Cork when captured off Martinique. This poor woman was thrown overboard, still alive, after twenty of his crew had raped her and broken her back.

Hanged alongside Sympson was the Orcadian Joseph Mansfield. This one-time highwayman had deserted from Woodes Rogers' naval escort HMS *Rose* and later joined Davis's pirate company on the *Buck* at Hispaniola. On the day of the momentous engagement with HMS *Swallow*, he was so badly inebriated below decks that he only managed to stagger onto the deck of the *Royal Fortune* to lead a boarding party with drawn cutlass and swearing after the fight was lost. He was aged 30 when the hangman's noose was tightened round his neck.

Dangling beside him were a fellow Orcadian, John Stephenson, and two Aberdonians, Peter Lesley and Israel Hynd. The 24-year-old Lesley had been a seaman on the *Onslow*. He had, very foolishly, decided to join the pirates just as the net was closing around them. A number of very Scottish-sounding characters stood beside him at the trial but whose origins, unfortunately, were not recorded by the surgeon Atkins. These include Robert Armstrong, Peter Cromby, Hugh Harris and William Macintosh (all hanged), Hugh Menzies (acquitted) and Thomas Ouchterlony (pardoned).

Armstrong was the only one of the whole group who was hanged from the yardarm of HMS *Weymouth* which was at anchor off Cape Coast Castle at the time. The navy claimed their right to hang him as he was a deserter from HMS *Rose*. It is an interesting aside that, of the *Weymouth*'s crew assembled to witness the punishment, Alexander Selkirk (Robinson Crusoe) was missing. Selkirk had only recently died while serving on the ship as an able seaman and had been buried at sea off the Guinea Coast.

The bodies of Sympson and Mansfield were among the eighteen chosen to be tarred and hung in chains on the three hills above the Cape Coast Castle. There they swung to the ocean breeze, rapidly rotting in the sweltering heat and humidity.

Among those released or pardoned were the three surgeons found on board Roberts's flotilla as forced men. It was rare for a pirate crew to let a surgeon or his mate go when they laid hands on them. Apart from injuries sustained in their chosen profession, they were invariably riddled with 'Guinea fever' and syphilis. Any surgeon who survived the close proximity to the pirates' diseases and random acts of violence, could only hope that his captors would be quickly hunted down.

Around this time, the Royal Colleges of Surgeons in Scotland (Edinburgh, Glasgow and Aberdeen) were churning out 80 per cent of Britain's qualified doctors. The dire lack of positions available at home meant that most were obliged to earn their living beyond their native shores. It comes, therefore, as no surprise that pirates laid hands on a number of them.

Dr Archibald Murray, surgeon on the *Buck* at the time of the pirate insurrection, endured his two-year captivity till he was finally released at Inveraray Jail. The same fate befell the 26-year-old Dr Robert Hunter of Kilmarnock. He was taken off the *Jeremiah & Anne* of London close to Bermuda by the pirate George Lowther and forced to serve on the *Happy Delivery* (ex-*Bumper* galley) for close to a year.

Lowther had been the second mate of the Royal Africa Company's *Bumper* dispatched with passengers and forty soldiers to re-garrison the fort on St James Island in the Gambia River after it was burnt by Davis. Hunter's release came in 1723 when Lowther was trapped while careening his vessel in a secluded cove on the small island of Blanquilla (North Venezuela) by the pirate hunter Captain Walter Moore on the South Sea Company armed sloop *Eagle*.

Lowther initially got away by climbing out of one of the stern windows, but was later found on the islet with his brains blown out and a discharged pistol by his side. One of Lowther's men who did make good his escape that day was the impressive-sounding Lancelot Johnston, previously from Galashiels. The rest of the crew, including the Scots, Edward McDonald and Andrew Hunter, were tried and hanged at St Kitts in March of 1724.

Lowther had previously forced the 25-year-old John Crawford, a Scots surgeon on the merchantman *Greyhound* of Boston taken off Honduras in January 1722. Her captain put up a stout defence for an hour before surrendering. For his defiance he and his officers were badly drubbed while the crew were wantonly cut about. Crawford was singled out for torture with lighted fuses between his fingers to reveal the whereabouts of some concealed gold dust. Lowther, no doubt, got wind of it from the first mate, Charles Harris, who had chosen to turn pirate and sign Articles. Before the vessel was set on fire, three other skilled men were also forced. One was the carpenter, David Lindsay, a 50-year-old Scot.

Lowther's former sailing partner, Edward Low, also forced and retained a young Scots surgeon on board his ship the *Fancy*. Dr John Hincher was a fine catch as he was a recent graduate of Edinburgh University. Low was a psychopath of the same order as Blackbeard and delighted in mutilating his victims and brutalising his crew.

Hincher is the most likely candidate for the unnamed drunken surgeon who was forced to stitch a severe cutlass wound to Low's face. During the operation Low took great exception to the poor quality of his handiwork, whereupon the surgeon struck him such a hard blow with his fist that the stitches burst, reopening the wound to expose his teeth, telling him to *stitch it himself!* This may have been the reason why Hincher was later transferred onto the prize *Rebecca* which Low had given to his newest recruit, the first mate Harris, as a consort to the *Fancy*.

When HMS *Greyhound* caught up with them in 1723, Low fled, abandoning Harris and the pirate crew on the *Rebecca* to their fate. At their trial in New Port, Rhode Island in July, Harris and twenty-three of his crew were convicted and condemned to hang. Hincher and another forced man from Edinburgh, the 17-year-old John Fletcher, were pardoned.

The sadistic Low was later bundled into a small boat by his own crew and cast adrift. He was picked up by a French warship and summarily hanged from the yardarm.

What drove men to sign Articles of Regulation and become Blades was usually a combination of the desire to escape cruelty at the hands of a ruthless and exploitative master, the lure of a decadent life – albeit a short one – and the prospect of treasure.

The first motive is best illustrated by the *Last Dying Words* of William Fly, one of the last pirates of the era to be hanged. He faced the noose at Boston on 12 July 1726, unrepentant and defiant to the last. The self-righteous and pompous Reverend Cotton Mathers, in company with the Reverend Benjamin

Colman, led the gaggle of ministers intent on extracting a last-minute confession from these godless men. They were astonished at Fly's utter lack of contrition or remorse when facing death.

In the highest cavalier fashion, he assisted the fumbling hangman to tie the appropriate knot. Thereafter, he proclaimed from the steps to the gallows that his fondest wish was that *all Masters of Vessels might take warning by the Fate of the Captain that he had murder'd, and to pay Sailors their wages when due, and to treat them better; saying, that their Barbarity to them made so many turn Pyrates.*

One of the men acquitted at this trial, eight days before, was the forced Scot, William Ferguson.

Howell Davis's conversion to piracy mirrors the pressures and abuses listed by Fly. Born to the sea, he made his last legal voyage as the first mate on the slaver *Cadogan* snow of Bristol under the ruthless Captain Skinner. Off Sierra Leone, the *Cadogan* was taken and plundered by Edward England.

A number of his pirate crew had served under Skinner and held a deep grievance against him. He had, apparently, turned them over to a naval press-gang as troublemakers and pocketed their wages after they had made a complaint. Unbeknown to Skinner, they later deserted and found their way to New Providence. Defoe records that as soon as the pirates boarded the *Cadogan* Skinner's old boatswain, probably John Taylor, confronted him: *Ah, Capt. Skinner! Is it you? The only Man I wish to see; I am much in your Debt, and now I shall pay all in your own coin.* He summoned the others who had been abused by him and after a vote, tied him to the capstan where they pelted him with broken wine bottles until he bled profusely. He was then severely lashed before being shot through the head and dumped overboard.

The testimony of the much-abused John Lazenby, the second mate forced from the *Cassandra* by England and Taylor, makes it certain that had Captain James Macrae been recaptured, he would have received similar treatment.

The attrition rate among the pirates to disease and mindless violence was such that skilled men were forced whenever they were captured. Howell Davis, as a first mate, was a prime candidate as he understood the art of navigation, which very few seamen then did. England had tried with death threats to get him to sign Articles but Davis steadfastly refused. England, admiring his pluck, wrote him a letter that gave him the looted *Cadogan* and what was left of its cargo, after which England departed to raid the Azores and went on to the Guinea Coast.

Davis took the *Cadogan* across the Atlantic to Barbados where his reward for his courageous stand was to be flung in prison for three months for consorting with pirates. Blacklisted by the local merchants thereafter, he resolved to join the pirates on New Providence at the first opportunity. He arrived on the island at the same time as Woodes Rogers.

Bartholomew 'Black Bart' Roberts embraced piracy in much the same way. He was the third mate on the slaver *Princess* of London when Howell Davis took her off Anamaboe in November 1719. He too refused to sign Articles but six weeks later, following the death of Davis, he had turned pirate. He declared himself a candidate for the vacant captaincy with the statement: *it is better to be a captain than a common man, since I have dipped my hands in muddy water and must be a pirate.*

Defoe reckoned that the secret of Roberts's spectacular success as a pirate captain – he took over 400 vessels – was that he strove to curb the destructive effect that habitual heavy drinking of punch had on his crew's cohesion and ability to fight. He was himself an avid tea-drinker and disciplinarian.

Arguably the best account of pirate behaviour is that of Captain William Snelgrove. He was taken prisoner after his slaver, the *Bird* galley, was boarded by pirates on April Fool's Day 1719. He was released, on a whim, a month later. In between times he had kept company with the forced cooper John Daniels of the *Loyalty* of Port Glasgow.

In his account, Snelgrove described the mayhem that followed the boarding of the *Bird* as she lay in the Sierra Leone River, by a long-boat party from Cocklyn's vessel. He claimed that he only escaped being killed during the first moments of the assault by the loyalty of his boatswain, who vouched for his good treatment of his crew. The late arrival of Davis's men turned the looting into a drunken orgy:

> *hoisted upon the Deck a great many half hogsheads of Claret and French Brandy: knock'd their Heads out, and dipp'd Canns and Bowls into them to drink out of: And in their wantonness threw full Buckets upon one another. And in the evening washed the Decks with what remained in the Casks. As to bottled Liquor, they would not give themselves the trouble of drawing the Cork out, but nick'd the Bottles, as they called it, that is, struck their necks off with a Cutlace.*

Roberts seems to have convinced himself that such indiscipline had played its part in the loss of the *Royal Rover* and the treasure he had left in Kennedy's care. Immediately afterwards, he wrote out these strict new Articles for his remaining crewmen to sign:

> I.   *Every Man has a Vote in Affairs of Moment; has equal Title to the fresh Provision, or strong Liquors, at any Time seized, & use them at pleasure, unless a Scarcity make it necessary, for the good of all, to vote a retrenchment.*

II. *Every Man to he called fairly in turn, by List, on Board of Prizes, because they were on the Occasions allow'd a Shift of Cloaths: But if they defrauded the Company to the Value of a Dollar, in Plat, Jewels or Money, Marooning to be their Punishment. If the Robbery was only between one another, they must content themselves with slitting the Ears and Nose of him that is guilty, and set him on Shore, not in an uninhabited Place, but somewhere, where he is sure to encounter hardships.*

III. *No Person to Game at Cards or Dice for Money.*

IV. *The Lights & Candles to be put out at eight o'Clock at Night: If any of the Crew, after that Hour, still remained inclined for Drinking, they were to do it on the open deck.*

V. *To keep their Pieces, Pistols & Cutlash, clean & fit for Service.*

VI. *No Boy or Woman to be allow'd amongst them. If any Man is found seducing any of the latter Sex, and carried her to Sea, disguised, he is to suffer Death.*

VII. *To Desert the Ship, or their Quarters in Battle, is punished with Death, or Marooning.*

VIII. *No striking one another on Board, but every Man's quarrels to be ended on Shore, at Sword & Pistol.*

IX. *No Man to talk of breaking up their Way of Living, till each had shared a £1000. If in order to this, any Man should lose a Limb, or become a Cripple in their Service, he was to have 800 dollars, out of the publick stock, and for lesser Hurts, proportionably.*

X. *The Captain and Quarter-master to receive two Shares of a Prize, the Master, Boatswain & Gunner, one Share and a half, and other Officers, one and a Quarter.*

XI. *The Musicians to have Rest on the Sabbath Day, but the other six Days & Nights none without special Favour.*

There was also an unwritten addendum – that no Irishman should ever again serve under his command.

Roberts also knew how to create an awe-inspiring personal image that struck terror in his victims and generated fierce loyalty in his men. At the moment of his death, on the quarterdeck of the *Royal Fortune*, he was dressed in a *rich crimson damask waistcoat and breeches, a red feather in his hat, a gold chain round his neck, with a diamond cross hanging to it, a sword in his hand and a pair of pistols hanging at the end of a silk sling, hung over his shoulder*. Lord Sympson was said to have been in tears when he fulfilled his captain's long-standing request that, should he be killed in battle, his body was to be immediately dropped over the side.

The same cannot be said for Bonnet's tormentor and tyrant, Edward 'Blackbeard' Teach. Though a highly skilled seaman, he kept his crew in terror of him with random acts of violence, usually following heavy drinking bouts. Occasionally he would kill or maim one of his crew – *lest they would forget who he was* – as with Israel Hands, crippled for life by a musket ball fired under the table.

Teach's *Journal* of his cruise on the sardonically named *Queen Anne's Revenge* gives some idea of the knife-edge existence his crew shared with him: *Rum all out. Our Company somewhat sober – A damn'd Confusion amongst us! Rogues plotting – great Talk of Seperation – so I look'd sharp for a prize … Took one with a great deal of liquor on Board, so kept the Company hot, damned hot, then all things went well again.* It was a rum-sodden Blackbeard who was, along with most of his crew, shot and hacked down in his famous final encounter with Lieutenant Maynard's squadron in the waters of the Ocracoke Inlet.

Because of their violent deaths, there was no opportunity for any official to enquire as to their origins. The only Scot that is known to have sailed with Blackbeard was William

Cunninghame, his master gunner. He had taken the pardon but later reneged when Governor Rogers looked to be losing control. He then joined Captain John Auger's company operating out of New Providence. Their pirating activities were quickly ended by Captain Hornigold, Woodes Rogers' very effective 'gamekeeper'. Cunninghame was one of those hanged at New Providence by order of Rogers as a show of strength to the local Brethren.

Unlike the summary trials meted out by Rogers and the panel of officers convened at Cape Coast Castle, the piracy trial heard before Lord James Graham sitting in Edinburgh followed due legal process. Detailed allegations and defences were lodged for each of the pirates captured from Walter Kennedy's crew off the *Eagle* in Craignish Loch. These offer a unique insight into the membership and doings of the pirate crews of Davis and Roberts.

All pleaded *defence of force* that they were not *Blades of Fortune* or *Standard pirates* (who had willingly signed Articles) but ordinary sailors who had in fear of death signed up. For *had the pirates taken it into their heads to enter into such Articles, whoever aboard the ship had refused to assent to them ... a Hatchet or Cutlace must have resolved their Fate; Whiping or Irons would have gone for nothing, when they were resolved to tye the Knot secure; Recusants behoved to be dispatch'd, that they might not tell tales.*

Each told their personal tale of capture and torture to the jury. 'Lord' Roger Hughes (Hews) acknowledged that he was a member of the nineteen crew of the *Buck* that first sailed her across the Atlantic from England with Governor Rogers. He claimed, however, that he was still sick with 'Guinea distemper' and below decks under Dr Murray's care, when Howell Davis led the pirates that took over the sloop at Hispaniola. Not being one of the Blades, he was confined to the hold at pistol point during the taking of prizes.

Richard Jones claimed that he was forced from the fourth prize, a Philadelphian vessel taken by Davis while still in the Caribbean. After he had surrendered, Davis's gunner maliciously slashed him across his leg with a cutlass before tying a rope round his middle and dragging him into the long-boat. The wound was so deep that it took six weeks of dressing in bandages by Dr Murray to heal.

On his recovery he made his bid to escape while the *Buck* was at St Nicholas, one of the Cape Verde Islands off the West African Coast. Pursued by Kennedy, he was eventually hunted down and recaptured sixteen miles inland. He desperately appealed to the local governor for protection, but this cry fell on deaf ears as the wily Kennedy (using his smattering of Portuguese) convinced the Governor that Jones was a deserter from one of the English slaving forts on the Guinea Coast. Once back on the *Buck*, Jones claimed he was severely lashed at the mast and never allowed ashore again.

All the other defendants told similar stories of random violence, mock executions and threats of marooning for refusing to fight or attempts at escape. William Green, a sailmaker on the *Guinea Hen* of Barbados, taken off the Isle of May, escaped only to be caught by 'the Moors' and handed back. For that he was slashed a few times before being whipped. He also recalled that some time later he refused to handle a pistol during an attack. Davis pressed him so hard to take it that the pistol went off, shooting a hole through Dr Murray's valuable medicine chest and breaking a number of bottles inside. For that he was brought to the mast and flogged to within an inch of his life.

Perhaps the saddest tale was that of the 16-year-old Hymen Saturly, who was taken off the *Jack* in the Sierra Leone River. This happened just before Davis, Cocklyn and La Bouche launched their attack on Bance Island fort. He managed to escape with some others and made it to the fort where they roused the garrison to their imminent danger. For the next twenty-four hours they helped fight off the pirates. When the fort was finally stormed by a landing party, he managed to flee upriver in a canoe.

Soon afterwards, he was captured by local natives and delivered back on board one of the pirate vessels. At Frenchman's Bay, in the estuary mouth, the pirates called in to divide their spoils, carouse and take on water. He then volunteered to go as the guide for the shore party as the area was heavily wooded. The pirates soon rumbled that his real intention was to attempt another escape and had him dragged back aboard where he was savagely whipped.

All these stories of desperate escapes and barbaric treatment did not impress the jury sitting in Edinburgh. They were all found guilty and, with the exception of the youth Saturly who was pardoned due to his age, were hanged on Leith Sands.

CHAPTER 8

Daniel Defoe,
Sir Walter Scott
& the Pirates

Defoe has been credited as the father of the 'adventure novel' and Scott the father of the 'Scottish novel'. Both shared a common interest in Scottish history and a particular fascination with the sordid exploits of Scottish rogues and pirates, at least one of whom, John Gow, the Orcadian pirate, was thoroughly investigated by both.

Daniel Foe (he later added the 'De' to his surname) was born to a dissenting Presbyterian family of butchers some time around 1660. He died 'of a lethargy' in 1731 in lodgings in Ropewalk Alley, Moorfields, a short distance from where he was born in East London. He had been, yet again, hiding out from his creditors. During his adult lifetime, the 'Golden Age of Piracy' had flourished, rampaged around the world and finally burned itself out.

Defoe's background is as shadowy as the rogues and villains he chose to write about. Bankrupted three times, he struggled to avoid debtors' prison while earning an erratic living as a poet, political satirist, propagandist, government spy, hack newspaper reporter and finally novelist. His bitter experience with the libel laws taught him to use the cover of a nom de plume or the anonymity of the unsigned 'True Account of'.

Whether or not Defoe wrote the *General History of the Robberies and Murders of the Most Notorious Pyrates* (1724) under the nom de plume Captain Charles Johnson, has been hotly contested ever since their names were first linked in 1932. Prior to that, the generally held assumption was that Johnson was a real captain, a man who had sailed with or knew the pirates intimately and who subsequently retired to write and publish his experiences. This was certainly the view of the pirate historian, Philip Gosse, in his foreword to a 1925 edition. This was the ninth edition, by which time the book had been sold in four different languages, a lasting testament to the durability of the public interest in pirates.

Unfortunately, there is not a trace of such a captain ever existing around the right historical period. This makes Johnston's existence dubious, as those who did make a good living from their buccaneering memoirs, such as the 'Devil's Mariner' William Dampier and his fellow adventurers William Hacke and Lionel Wafer, all knew each other and were celebrities on the fringe of fashionable London society. They left corroborating eye-witness accounts and a trail of personal and official documentation by which to authenticate their existence and verify their claims.

None of these authors can possibly be the writer of what has since come to be known as 'Johnson's Pirates'. All were long dead by the time the two hell-cats Anne Bonny and Mary Read (recorded in the first edition) were tried in Jamaica in 1720. Of the first wave of buccaneer captains of the Golden Age of Piracy, only Woodes Rogers was in London at the time of the release of the first edition in 1724. That he is the mysterious Captain Johnson is possible, but highly unlikely, as he is known to have published only once, and then under his own name, back in 1712. Moreover, he would never have made the small discrepancies in dates, names and places that riddle the section on New Providence and the pirates.

The other highly unlikely candidate, who hardly deserves a mention, is the actor and hack playwright Charles Johnson. He lived in London around the time and penned the play *The Successful Pyrate* which was first performed at the Theatre Royal in Drury Lane in 1713. This tale was loosely based on the life and adventures of the first great Indian Ocean pirate Henry Avery; hence the possibility that he might be the author of 'Johnson's Pirates'. However, all his other dramatic works were on wholly unrelated subjects. Indeed, there is no evidence to connect this famously overweight thespian and notorious plagiarist with the sea or pirates.

Defoe, on the other hand, fits the profile perfectly. Indeed, it is somewhat astonishing, given his propensity to write under pen-names and his known interests, that his name was not connected with Captain Johnson earlier. He had originally intended to enter the Church but chose instead to be a merchant in overseas trade. His short career in mercantile speculation ended in bankruptcy, leaving him with a colossal debt of £17,000. It did, however, bring him into contact with sea captains and their accounts of pirates. He had other connections with the sea: his sister had married a shipwright and he is thought to have known Woodes Rogers when he resided in London.

Furthermore, during his numerous visits to Scotland, from 1706 onwards, he would have followed the example of the vast majority of gentlemen travellers and sailed from London to Leith. By all accounts the (at times) hair-raising passages on the fast sailing smacks which regularly plied this route provided many an attentive passenger with an education in practical seamanship. He was, therefore, well informed on maritime and plantation matters and understood the principles of handling a ship at sea. These details add that touch of authenticity to the accounts of 'Johnson's Pirates' and underpin the original assumption that the author must have been a real sea captain. As all circumstantial and stylistic evidence point to Defoe, it is my opinion that he is the author of the *General History of Pyrates*. The first, leather-bound, edition of which went on sale from Charles Rivington's bookshop in St Paul's, London, in May 1724.

Defoe developed his interest in maritime low life during his six-year editorial collaboration with John Applebee. This publisher was particularly noted for his *Confessions* and short biographies of notorious criminals and miscreants.

Their relationship was struck up when Defoe's career as government spy and political satirist (he wrote under such pseudonyms as 'Quaker', 'Scots gentleman', 'Jacobite rebel' and 'Turkish spy') came to an abrupt end in 1718. He was rumbled for writing simultaneously for the Whig *Whitehall Evening Post* and the Tory *Weekly Journal or Secondary Post*. Only the previous year he was regularly publishing (anonymously) in the Jacobite *Mist's Weekly Journal*. When this became public knowledge, he lost the trust of all combatants in the political arena. Defoe's services as a political *agent provocateur* and 'spin doctor' were summarily dispensed with. Indeed, the hoodwinked editor of *Mist's Weekly Journal*, on hearing of Defoe's duplicity, threatened to pursue and murder him.

Defoe was approaching sixty when he started his new commission with *Applebee's Original Weekly Journal*. This involved visiting Newgate and Marshalsea prisons to glean the necessary gruesome details and the woeful tales expected by its readership.

He was, of course, no stranger to the inside of a prison cell, having been arrested twice for libel. This time, however, he came into direct contact with the worst of London's underworld – prostitutes, highway robbers and pirates.

His key contact in Newgate Prison was the Reverend Paul Lorrain. For twenty years Lorrain had served as chaplain to the condemned – the 'Ordinary' – in the prison. A major part of his job was to interrogate the wretches in the hope that by confronting them with their past sins, they would repent and so become one of 'Lorrain's Saints'. He then accompanied them on their last cart ride through the streets of London, lined with jeering mobs, to the gallows. Pirate executions were particularly well attended and attracted vast crowds along the route to Execution Dock, Wapping. Many shouted taunts at the doomed pirate to throw them 'pieces of eight' as he passed.

Lorrain also had a profitable sideline – writing 'broadsheets' that sold for a penny or two on the streets just before or immediately after an execution. These recorded the purported *Confessions* heard by him in the condemned man's cell the night before, or the *Last Dying Words* gathered from the foot of the hangman's ladder. Indeed, Lorrain would have been a prime contender for the credit of writing 'Johnsons Pirates', had he not died in 1719. Defoe had full access to these broadsheets (collectively known as the *Newgate Calendar*), as Applebee was Lorrain's official printer.

Another source for Defoe was the trials themselves, which were open to the public. The trial of Walter Kennedy heard at the Old Bailey in 1721 described the fate of 'Black Bart' Roberts's treasure and the episode at Loch Craignish in Argyll-shire which Defoe briefly mentions. It would, however, seem certain that he had not attended the earlier trial of Kennedy's crew in Edinburgh (1719). None of the extensive and new details of the pirate activities of Davis and Roberts available from that trial are evident in 'Johnson's Pirates'. Indeed, if Defoe had relied on the contemporary newspapers – the *London Gazette*, *Edinburgh Evening Courant* and *Edinburgh Gazette* – to cover that trial for him, he would have gleaned only the barest statements as to their arrest and execution.

The testimonies of the Craignish pirates and that of the prosecution witnesses serve, therefore, as a unique independent verification of the authenticity of 'Johnson's Pirates'. The conclusion is that Defoe's general story-line on the spread of piracy out of New Providence is very close to that given in evidence in Edinburgh. Similarly, his specific details of the actions and character of the major pirates involved – Davis, Roberts, Antis and Kennedy – are a very good match.

Dates of events, however, slip by a month in some instances and there are a few discrepancies between the witness statements and Defoe's account in 'Johnson's Pirates', the principal one being that he states that Dennis Topping (one of the six pirate 'Lords' with Davis at the taking of the *Buck*) was killed boarding the Portuguese bullion galleon *Sacrada Familia* off Brazil. In fact, Topping was very much alive and well when he stood trial for piracy at Edinburgh almost a year later. Indeed, Topping ('Toppen' on the list of accused) was one of the fortunate seven who were acquitted on the grounds that he was forced from the slaver *Morrice* at Anamaboe and was never a Blade. Topping is thought to have returned to London, where most retiring pirates headed, on his release from Edinburgh Castle. It is little wonder that Defoe chose to hide behind a pen-name with such rogues at large.

Defoe was ideally suited for his new line of work. A lifetime as a hand-to-mouth political journalist had equipped him with an eye for a story. His distinctive direct reporting style worked well with this type of seedy material and publisher. He was, by then, an expert in the use and abuse of facts with which to spin a moral tale.

Shortly after he embarked on this new career, he decided to try his hand at novel writing. His first effort, *Robinson Crusoe*, published in April 1719, was an instant success. This immortal tale of marooning was based on the experiences of Alexander Selkirk of Upper Largo, Fife. Selkirk, the world's most famous castaway, had been rescued from his self-imposed exile by Woodes Rogers. Rogers was cruising off the Chilean coast on the *Duke*, with Dampier as his pilot on the *Dutchess*, in search of Spanish prizes when he called into Selkirk's chosen home – the island of Juan Fernandez.

Rogers had published his account of this epic voyage, *A Cruising voyage round the World ... begun 1708 and finished 1711 ... an account of Alexander Selkirk's living alone four years and four months in an island*, in London in 1712. This provided Defoe with the raw material for his most famous character. Whether he ever met Selkirk has never been established. Selkirk returned to London on Rogers' *Duke* before Defoe was dispatched to Scotland for the second time. It is, therefore, quite probable that they did, for a mariner who had sailed with Dampier and Rogers was a celebrity in London's world of commerce and shipping. Selkirk later died while serving on board a British warship off the Guinea Coast and was buried at sea.

More to the point, Rogers was back in London in 1721. Having rid New Providence of its pirates, he had fallen foul of the same brand of skulduggery that ended the careers of two other governors, Lord Archibald Hamilton and James Macrae. Rogers' twenty-one-year Crown lease of the Bahamas was rescinded and he was recalled under a cloud and close to bankruptcy. Indeed, he spent some time in debtors' prison before he eventually cleared his name and regained his position as governor, returning to the Bahamas in 1728.

During Rogers' sojourn in London, to canvass their Lordships of the Board of Trade for justice and recompense, Defoe had ample opportunity to renew his acquaintance with him. It is virtually inconceivable that Defoe – the man who wrote *Robinson Crusoe* – would not have used this opportunity to hear at first-hand Rogers' account of his rescue of Selkirk from his island and of the spread of piracy and the evil-doings of the rogues he expelled from New Providence.

In the adept hands of Defoe, such privileged information was collated and reworked to suit his own ends. He had learned from his time with Applebee that what sold well was heaps of gratuitous violence and an occasional incident of sexual abuse, set in wondrous and wild places. The moral message was usually hammered home with the inevitable grisly ending for the wrongdoers.

The perfect vehicle for his style was the fake autobiography complete with *The Authentic Account of,* cover. It was a winning formula that he repeated with *The Further Adventures of Robinson Crusoe, Moll Flanders, Roxana,* and the pirate tale *The Adventures of Captain Singleton.* Stories of the adventures of pirates committing crimes on the grandest scale and a harlot's progress to the New World greatly appealed to the scandal-mongering and hedonistic society of Hogarth's London.

The known world of the early eighteenth century was then expanding geographically at breakneck speed along with debates on social values and political outlook. The philosophers mused on the pirate phenomenon – an anarchic group made up of desperate individuals waging war on all society, yet a brotherhood tied by their own Articles of Regulation on their floating democracies. Defoe's description of the settlement of Liberteria on Madagascar founded by a pirate named Mission – a proto-socialist commune which even forbade the planting of hedges between houses – was almost certainly one of his inventions aimed at intriguing his readership.

As the 'Age of Reason' blossomed in the sciences and humanities, so the Church's traditional monopoly on the instruction of individual morality was challenged. Pirates and highwaymen, by breaking the rules of society and paying the ultimate price, were a fashionable humanist alternative to the biblical parables of divine retribution. Even the morally righteous were intrigued by the sheer audacity, scale of wickedness and marvellous feats of seamanship of the Black Flag pirates.

In his extended Volume II of the *General History of Pyrates* (published in 1728) Defoe heavily indulged in moralising on the hypocrisies of the society of his day. This work reported mostly on the lives of the first generation of pirates – those raiding between 1695 and 1716. It was, therefore, based much more on hearsay and legend and less on contemporary accounts. Defoe has Avery, the man who took the fabulous treasure from the Great Mogul's ship, swindled out of his diamonds by local merchants in Barnstaple and dying a pauper without leaving the means to pay for his own coffin. He also took the liberty of inventing three fictitious pirates – Mission, Cornelius and Lewis – as vehicles for his sermonising.

Tinkering and embellishing the facts was a hallmark of Defoe's work. According to his own (unreliable) memoirs he was a politically active dissenter at the very start of the revolt against Catholic King James. He claimed to have served on the losing side during the Monmouth Rebellion. Somehow he managed to escape the field on his stampeding horse and so evaded the clutches of 'Hanging Judge' Jeffreys.

It would seem likely that he transposed his own experience to dramatise one of the key scenes in the story of the pirate Bartholomew Roberts. This is when 'Lord' Sympson begrudgingly withdrew his candidacy for the vacant captaincy of the *Royal Rover* after the death of Howell Davis. He credits the bigoted young Scotsman with the sour aside that *he did not care who they chose Captain, so it was not a papist, for against them he conceiv'd an irreconcileable Hatred, for that his father had been a Sufferer in Monmouth's Rebellion.*

Defoe's long association with Scotland came about as a consequence of his brushes with the Establishment. This close relationship had started well enough. Commencing in 1691 he wrote some favourably received pamphlets. His long poetic eulogy, *The True Born Englishman*, in praise of the new King William was highly popular in its day.

He later, however, got into serious trouble with the high Tories. In 1703, he published the satirical pamphlet *The Shortest Way With Dissenters*. This tract lampooned the Tories' hard-line stance: *'Tis vain to trifle in this matter. The light foolish handling of them by mulcts, fines, etc., 'tis their glory and advantage. If the gallows instead of the Counter, and the Gallies [slave galleys] instead of fines were the reward for going to a conventicle, to preach or hear, there would not be so many sufferers.* When it was realised that the 'high flyer Tory' author was the jumped-up dissenter Defoe, the Earl of Nottingham (Secretary of State and champion of the high Tories) made it his business to have him tracked down. For this piece of ironic mimicry Defoe was imprisoned, convicted and sentenced to stand in the pillory three times. This led to his second bankruptcy in 1704 and paved the way for his recruitment as a government agent.

In 1706 Robert Harley, Secretary of State for England, sent Defoe to Scotland as a propagandist. His mission for 'Robin the Trickster' was to write pamphlets to sway public opinion towards accepting the Act of Union. He later claimed that in this *special service … I had to run as much risk of my life as a grenadier upon a counterscarp*. Nevertheless, he churned out a prodigious amount of tracts across the spectrum of topics related to the Union for his master.

When Harley was dismissed from government in 1708, Defoe was retained by the Queen's chief minister, 'Clockwork Godolphin'. Godolphin was a moderate Tory who tolerated Defoe's pro-Whig Review newspaper, in which Defoe continued to write thrice weekly. It was during this term of employment that he published his *History of the Union* (1709) in which he reported on the political implications of the piracy trial of Captain Green and his crew at Edinburgh four years earlier. By 1710 Harley was back in office and Defoe's pen was again gainfully employed for the Whigs.

In 1714 he was again in prison for libel. It was a short interlude as he was soon freed on the orders of Lord Townsend, the latest Secretary of State. Townsend urgently needed Defoe's skills as an impersonator and his knowledge of Scotland to infiltrate the Jacobite circles that had gone underground since the failed 'Fifteen

Rebellion'. During this mission (1716–20) Defoe toured Scotland extensively, acquiring a very good geographic knowledge of the remote parts of the region.

Defoe put this to good use when relating the various locations surrounding the comings and goings of the pirate John Gow in Orcadian waters. His story initially appears in a thick pamphlet, *An Account of the Conduct and Proceeding of the late John Gow alias Smith Captain of the Late Pirates Executed for Murther and Piracy*. It was unsigned, but there can be no dispute as to his authorship as his editor-to-be (after 1726), Mr Lee, cross-referenced 'Gow' with 'Defoe' in his personal catalogue.

This pamphlet was released by Applebee on 11 June 1725, the day of Gow's execution. The trial had started only seventeen days earlier and so it was a classic piece of opportunistic courtroom journalism. It was never reprinted, for soon afterwards the third edition of *Johnson's Pirates* appeared. This edition contained the first major change in content with the inclusion of a new section, 'The Life of Captain Gow', together with a lesser essay on the Irish pirate Roche.

One hundred years later Sir Walter Scott was involved in a scheme to edit Defoe's great legacy to Scottish affairs and history, a veritable mountain of pamphlets, tracts and commentaries. He was certainly aware of his work on Gow, as well as his essays, *Scottish Rogues*, in which he took a keen interest. This latter work included a description of a contemporary of Gow, the cattle thief and proscribed outlaw Rob Roy Macgregor. Sir Walter Scott rehabilitated the wild robber Rob Roy by raising him to the status of a romantic legend caught up in the changing turbulent world of the Highlands after the Fifteen Rebellion.

Scott's interest in Gow was stimulated by his voyage in 1814 to Orkney on board the sloop *Pharos*, belonging to the Commisioner for Northern Lights. Britain was then at war with Napoleon's empire and America. The risk of enemy privateers in northern waters was very high, so the sloop was armed and escorted by the sloop-of-war HMS *Spitfire* when she left Leith. The *Spitfire* soon detached herself as she was ordered to join up with the light frigate HMS *Alexandria* in the hunt for the elusive American super-frigate USS *President*.

Once the *Pharos* was in the Pentland Firth, her watch sighted a large vessel in the distance. It was USS *President* making her way through the passage en route to intercepting the British Archangel convoys off Spitsbergen. It is an interesting conjecture to consider what would have been the impact on the Scottish novel had Commodore John Rodgers taken Scott prisoner that day and carried him off to America.

As it was, Scott was landed safely on Orkney and went in search of the traditions surrounding the local pirate. At Stromness, Gow's home-port, he sought out the ancient Bessie Millie. She was a wizened old lady who 'sold winds' to anxious mariners for a sixpence from her house perched high above the harbour. Approaching her hundredth year, she regaled Scott with the tale of Gow, whom she claimed to have known when she was a child. Moving on to Kirkwall he visited the Sheriff-Substitute, Mr Peterkin, and pestered him to prepare a full account of Gow's crimes and arrest, even though it all happened ninety years in the past.

After a gestation period of seven years the novel *The Pirate* was published. In the interim Scott had fully absorbed the wild and beautiful seascapes of the Shetlands and Orkney Isles into his writing, with most of the plot takes place at the former location. As to characters, Scott utilised very little of the unsavoury John Gow in his pirate character Captain Cleveland. Bessie Millie, however, had left her impression, as he gave her a cameo appearance as 'Norna of the Fitful Head'. Only in the later part of the story does the plot transfer back to Orkney and the real incidents first reported by Defoe, principally the abduction and abuse of the two local women by Gow's crew and the taking of a hostage.

The novel was well received in its time but has since fallen from favour with the reader and critic alike. The master pirate storyteller, Robert Louis Stevenson, later denounced it as a *ragged, ill-written book*. Others, admirers of Scott's vivid and atmospheric settings, continue to find great merit in the work.

The Earlier Wave of Pirates in the Indian Ocean, 1695–1705

CHAPTER 9

The Company of Scotland & the Madagascan Pirates

On 18 August 1696, a Royal Proclamation was nailed to the 'mercat cross' on the Royal Mile in Edinburgh, and at the major ports throughout Scotland, for *Apprehending Henry Every, alias Bridgeman and Sundry other Pirates*. The Lords Justices sitting in London promised to pay £500 sterling for information leading to the arrest of the great pirate captain and £50 for each of the *English Men, Scots Men and foraigners, to the number of one hundred and thirty* that were his crew. This reward matched that already offered (in rupees) by the Honourable East India Company the previous month.

Captain 'Long Ben' Avery (or Every) was the first European pirate to round the Cape of Good Hope to raid in the Indian Ocean and Red Sea, using Isle de Johanna and Madagascar as his bases. In the space of less than two years his exploits had, as Defoe put it, *made a great noise in the world* that shook the very foundations of the British presence in India.

At the centre of this great furore was the taking of the Mogul's greatest ship, the *Gang-i-Sawai*, returning from Mocha in the Red Sea with 600 pilgrims from Mecca. This massive and heavily armed vessel was captured after a savage two-hour battle during which a number of Avery's crew on his ship the *Fancy* were killed.

On finally boarding his victim, he exacted a terrible retribution on these 'heathens' that was barbaric even by the standards of cruelty of the day. The male passengers, many high-ranking court officials, were tortured to reveal their hidden gold and silver before being butchered.

The women found below decks, many related to the Great Mogul Aurungzeeb, were treated likewise. Some chose to jump over the side to their deaths; others killed themselves with hidden daggers rather than face the orgy of rape that followed. Those women who did not die from their injuries sustained during this brutal ordeal, were kept as captives for the crew's amusement after the *Gang-i-Sawai* was finally cast adrift. Legend has it that Avery retained the granddaughter of Aurungzeeb as a wife.

It is little wonder that the Great Mogul raged against the Europeans in his Indian Empire. Such was his wrath that many officers of the English East India Company were imprisoned and a few executed over the following year. Once his anger had subsided and they were released, new restrictions were applied whereby they were forbidden to carry arms or display their national flags on their vessels. These measures were also extended to the Dutch and French factories.

To break the deadlock, the besieged Governor of Bombay offered to deploy a number of his armed East Indiamen – at full cost to the Company – as escorts to the Mocha fleets. He went further and commissioned the independent Scots merchant adventurer, Captain Alexander Hamilton, to make pre-emptive strikes against the native pirate nests along the Malabar Coast and the Persian Gulf. He also worked with his erstwhile rival French and Dutch counterparts to raise the fortune in compensation needed to placate the Mogul for his loss.

As the officers of the East India Company clawed their way back into favour and strove to avert the Company's extinction in India, its directors in London joined those of the Royal Africa Company to petition King William's government for respite. They demanded that immediate action be taken to clear out the nests of pirates that were now settling in their droves on Madagascar after Avery's sensational success. The Crown's response was to apply the 'carrot and stick' strategy (its first use since Elizabethan times). This entailed a general pardon for all but a few of the pirate captains operating east of the Cape of Good Hope, backed up by a small naval expedition to Madagascar.

Tremendous pressure was also brought to bear on the Crown to terminate the newest rival to the English trading monopolies: *The Company of Scotland, trading to Africa and the East Indies*. Usually referred to in English indictments as the 'Scots African Company', it had been set up in 1694 by a Scottish Act of Parliament during William's absence on military campaigns in the Low Countries.

The English Companies claimed that their new Scots rival had immediately set about recruiting large numbers of Avery's old pirate crew from their bolt-holes in Ireland and around the ports of Europe. Indeed, they insisted the Scots already had his old pilot safely in Edinburgh, where he was advising their directors on piratical schemes. Such was their concern that the English Lords Justices had a number of Avery's men tracked down and dragged from the alehouses of Dublin to be interrogated on the matter. The great buccaneer William Dampier was also summoned and questioned in London as to his links with the Scots Company.

In the meantime, the arch-pirate Avery got away 'Scot free' with over half a million pounds in gold, silver and diamonds. He had slipped away from his cruising partner, Thomas Tew, soon after the looting of the *Gang-i-Sawai* and headed for New Providence in the Bahamas. There he disbanded his crew. Some chose to head for America, others for Europe. Avery was last heard of landing from a New Providence sloop some miles north-west of Londonderry in Ireland. From there, according to one of his crew who was arrested, he intended to cross over to Scotland as 'Captain Bridgeman' on his way south to his retirement as an inconspicuous country gentleman of wealth.

The proclamation and its rewards for his capture yielded nothing. If anything, it served to promote the legend and inadvertently advertised the benefits of piracy. The public were advised that Avery and twenty-five named men from his crew, all *hainous and Notorious Offenders ... may be Probably known and Discovered by the Great Quantities of Persian and Indian Gold and Silver which they have with them.*

In getting away with the crime of the century, he immediately became the role model for all those who sailed under the Black Flag. Indeed, his spectacular cruise did much to trigger the 'Golden Age of Piracy' that held sway for the next thirty years. His awesome reputation is evident from the fact that the pirate John Taylor, who attacked Macrae on the *Cassandra* at Isle de Johanna fifteen years later, had renamed his vessel *Fancy* in his honour. The sadist Edward Low also emulated Avery by regularly indulging in the torture of his victims, cutting off the ears and noses of any unfortunate Spaniards who fell into his hands.

The lure of pirate gold and silver also attracted those who embarked upon privately sponsored 'pirate-chasing'. This quasi-public service was particularly attractive to members of the ruling Establishment with access to royal commissions. The opportunity seemed ideal as the renewed war with France had taken up most of the available naval resources.

The idea struck a particular chord with the newly appointed and self-righteous Governor of New York and New England, the Earl of Bellomont. This Irish peer had yet to sail to America as the replacement for the notoriously corrupt Governor Fletcher. Fletcher had taken a massive bribe from Thomas Tew to grant him a pardon and liberty to settle and sell his ill-gotten booty at New York.

Bellomont's new scheme to end piracy in the Red Sea and Indian Ocean, while making a handsome profit on his own account, was initially hatched by Colonel Livingston of New York, who happened to be in London at the time. His concept was as simple as it was appealing: a large powerful well-armed vessel with a large crew of war-hardened veterans would sail to Madagascar under dual privateering and pirate-hunting commissions. So empowered, her master could make prize those vessels caught sailing under the protection of the French flag while pursuing pirates of all nationalities.

The glittering lure of relieving pirates of their plunder attracted a number of Bellomont's powerful Whig friends as silent partners: Sir John Somers, then Keeper of the Great Seal; the Duke of Shrewsbury, the Secretary of State; the Earl of Romney, Master of the Royal Ordnance; and Sir Edward Russell (later Lord Orford), First Lord of the Admiralty. Livingston's fateful choice of captain for this money-spinning venture was the one-time privateering master and respected family man, Captain William Kidd, born in Dundee and resident of New York.

The tragic tale of Captain Kidd and the cruise of the *Adventure* galley rightfully belongs in the annals of privateering. It cannot be denied that he had the worst of luck and a mutinous crew during his three-year cruise (1696–9). He could have weathered all this had he not compromised his captaincy by a number of irresponsible acts which crossed the fine line that separates a privateer from a pirate.

He took only two vessels in all that time. Both were Moorish vessels which he approached under the ruse of flying the French flag. In this way he seized the great *Quedah Merchant* heading from Bengal for Surat with a rich cargo, which included seventy chests of opium belonging to Armenian merchants residing in Surat.

The capture took place on 30 January 1697, ten leagues off Cutsheen. Kidd ran in under French colours and her Dutch captain responded by sending over an old French-speaking gunner, posing as the captain, with their French passes. It was then common practice for neutrals to carry a set of passes from each of the warring European nations. At this, Kidd hoisted his English flag and declared the vessel lawful prize, to the great consternation of the Armenian owners who were on board.

Kidd refused a ransom of 30,000 rupees and decided, very foolishly, to escort his great prize to the pirates' lair of St Mary's Isle to divide the spoils. Once there, most of his disgruntled crew deserted him and joined up with Robert Culliford. This 'privateer-turned-pirate' was in harbour at the time with the *Mocha* frigate, an English East Indiaman he had recently taken and renamed the *Resolution*.

With only thirteen men remaining loyal to him, and receiving death threats from his deserters should he attempt anything against Culliford, Kidd was forced to barricade himself in the great cabin of the *Quedah Merchant* with forty muskets. From there he was unable to intervene as his badly leaking *Adventure* galley was left to sink at her mooring.

Abandoned by his officers, Kidd compromised himself in his need to find a crew to sail home with. This he did by coming to an amicable agreement of mutual co-existence with Captain Culliford. The two men – the supposed 'pirate-chaser' and the pirate – raised their glasses of bombo in convivial toasts to each other. Kidd gave Culliford ammunition, two cannons and money in return for Culliford's goodwill in fitting out the *Quedah Merchant* for a transatlantic crossing.

This deal got back to the ears of the agents of the East India Company in Bombay and, inevitably, to London. The directors immediately made it their business to have Kidd's name added to Avery's as one of only three pirates who were not to be granted the new pardon.

When Kidd finally made it back to Anguilla in the Leeward Islands of the West Indies in April 1699, he heard for the first time about the storm his escapades had raised. Indeed, the local island governors had been ordered by royal decree to apprehend him on sight on charges of piracy.

Faced with the prospect of hanging, many of his crew were for returning to Madagascar and turning pirate. He, however, clung to the belief that, with his powerful backers and his royal commissions, all could be explained away as simple errors of judgement or acts of expediency taken under dire circumstances many thousands of miles away in remote places.

Leaving the *Quedah Merchant* in the Higuey River at Hispaniola, he bought a small sloop, the *Antonio*, and made his way to New York to plead his case with his main promoter. On

3 July 1699 Bellomont finally heard his tale and took the French passes from him. Kidd's logbook had been missing since the *Adventure* galley sank at St Mary's Isle. So Bellomont insisted that he write a full account of his cruise, complete with a list of the booty taken and where he had buried it. Bellomont had already decided to distance himself from what was rapidly escalating into a national scandal. Three days later, he had Kidd arrested *as a most abandon'd villain* and, along with his crew found on the *Antonio*, clapped in irons.

By the time Kidd finally arrived back in the Thames, on board HMS *Advice* on 11 April 1700, he was a broken man, having spent nearly a year in solitary confinement. Taken upriver on the royal yacht *Katherine* under a close military guard, he was already a public spectacle when he entered Newgate Prison.

By now, the whole of London was awash with rumours and conspiracy theories. Captain Kidd's acts of piracy had been committed under royal commissions and for the financial benefit of high-ranking members of the Whig administration. At one stage the King himself seemed implicated. The Tory opposition, exulting in the scandal, intervened to made quite sure that there was to be no quick trial by which Bellomont and his friends could contrive an acquittal.

After yet another year in solitary confinement, during which time he was denied clothing, exercise, paper and pen and legal advice, Kidd was brought before the House of Commons in March 1701. In front of the assembled House, an attempt was made to badger him into implicating his partners in his venture, with a view to impeaching them. This he naïvely refused to do, claiming that, as he had done nothing wrong, they had nothing to answer for. As one weary Tory politician put it: *I thought him a knave. I now know him to be a fool as well.* This had been his last chance to bargain for a pardon. Afterwards all and sundry washed their hands of this pirate and left him for the courts to deal with.

The night before his appearance before the High Court of Admiralty of England, on 7 May 1701, the defence lawyers appointed on his behalf finally visited him in his cell. They told him that he faced six charges against which he would have to conduct own defence. He was aghast to find that the first was that of murder.

The incident this indictment referred to had happened just after the taking the *Quedah Merchant*. Kidd had endured a series of confrontations with his rabble-rousing and mutinous gunner, William Moore. This time Kidd snapped and threw an iron-hooped bucket at him that fractured the gunner's skull, causing his death a few hours later. In any other court of this period, this act of manslaughter (given the circumstances of a master facing down a mutineer) would have been deemed justifiable. Not permitted to call witnesses in his defence, the abandoned Kidd fumbled his case and the suitably guided jury took only one hour to find him guilty.

For the already doomed man, the outcome of the other five charges of piracy was a formality. Even so, his trial was woefully compromised by the mysterious disappearance of the two French passes taken from the *Quedah Merchant* and given to Bellomont. Their production in court would probably have vindicated his claim that she was a lawful prize taken in time of war or at least that he had acted, albeit foolishly, in good faith.

Kidd went to the gallows at the Old Stairs, Wapping, reeling drunk and fervently denying that he had ever committed an act of murder or piracy. His body was later hung in chains at Tilbury Point. His buried treasure, recovered from Long Island and conveyed with him on HMS *Advice*, was too tainted by the scandal to be acquired by the usual office-bearers. Instead, the newly enthroned Queen Anne gifted this sum to the new Hospital for Seamen that had recently been installed in her old palace at Greenwich.

Kidd's commanding place in the public's imagination then, as now, had little to do with great swashbuckling deeds or Black Flag piracy. Indeed, throughout his extended cruise of the Indian Ocean he had steadfastly refused his crew's demand to turn pirate and loot all vessels they encountered. His enduring fame is sustained by the public's eternal fascination with the fact that he buried most of his treasure on an island.

During the three-year cruise of the *Adventure* galley, Madagascar had blossomed into the greatest pirate haven for companies raiding in the Indian Ocean and Red Sea. Following Avery's example, pirate settlements sprang up at different locations around this giant island. The best known were at St Mary's Isle in the north-east, Maritan, Port Dauphin and Charnock's Point further down the east coast, and St Augustine and New Mathelage on the west coast. These were little more than hut villages fortified against attack from the sea and landward raids by the incessantly warring natives. When not pirating, many inhabitants of these stockades indulged in slaving or hired themselves out as mercenaries to the feuding local chiefs.

While all pirates lusted after readily disposable gold and silver coins and bullion, much of their booty was in the form of luxurious silks, damasks, ceramics and the spices of the East. Visitors to St Mary's Isle brought back tales of beaches littered with discarded bales and broached chests of great value – had they reached their intended European markets.

It did not take long for the more adventurous European and American merchants to perceive these settlements as emporia, places where the plundered riches of the East could be had for a cask of rum or a barrel of gunpowder or a pair of shoes. There was also the prospect of slaving on the East African coast, which lay beyond the writ of the Royal Africa Company's monopoly.

Scots traders had been preparing for such a venture ever since Avery captured the *Gang-i-Sawai*. In that year, Glasgow's merchants took their first practical step to enter the African trade by granting a city burgess ticket to the Englishman Captain Davies as *a person qualified to be useful to this burgh in voyages to Africa and America*. This coincided with the Company of Scotland's grandiose plan to found a Scots colony at Darien on the Isthmus of Panama. The public's imagination was immediately swept up with this scheme, as were most of the disposable resources of the diminutive Scots nation.

By early 1699, however, the first news of major setbacks at the fledgling colony was filtering back, shattering any prospect of a return on the monies already committed. With expenditure still soaring as preparations for the second expedition continued, the Company scrabbled for other ways to generate desperately needed revenue. They looked to utilise the Company's last remaining corporate asset, the 'Letters Patent' granted under their founding Act of the Scottish Parliament. These appeared to provide the legal cover under which small individual ventures could be sent out into the trading preserves of the English Companies.

Trading to the East offered the greatest prospect of high returns. To prepare the ground for such new ventures, the

Company instructed their principal captain, James Gibson (then in Amsterdam fitting out their newest warship the *Rising Sun*), to open negotiations with the Armenian merchants. His contact was Martin Gregory, a merchant well-connected with those trading in Surat and some of whose goods Captain Kidd had recently robbed from the *Quedah Merchant*.

It was realised that engaging in such a joint venture to Surat would be taken as a direct challenge to the English East India Company's monopoly. As the Scots Company's armed forces were over-committed elsewhere, it was decided to circumnavigate this threat and trade directly with China.

The Eastern hopes of the Company rested with the ship *Speedwell* (250 tons) which had just returned from Darien under Captain John Campbell. The Company's Articles of Agreement with Campbell and his chief supercargo, Robert Innes, were as ambitious as they were fastidious: *you are to make the best of your way for Macow [Macao], where when it pleases God you arrive, dispatch your boat with some persons that can speak Spanish or Portuguese to the City of Canton to invite some merchants down in order to treat with the Mandarin to obtain trade.* Much ink and paper was wasted on petty instructions as to who was allowed to sit at the captain's table during the voyage and how best to pack silk and tea.

Later that year, the solitary *Speedwell*, after fitting out at Leith, cleared from the Clyde for the Far East. The Company's last instructions were that they were to make for the Straits of Sunda and the Dutch conclave of Batavia on Java. There they were to trade for pepper and then proceed to Macao and Canton to exchange this cargo for silk, tea, porcelain and sugar. After this, they were to proceed to the Cape of Good Hope where instructions would be waiting on where to go next, depending on the war situation in Europe.

The primary target of this venture was almost achieved: the *Speedwell* got within ten leagues of Macao before she was driven back by a typhoon. During her second attempt, her hull was severely damaged by storms, so that she had to be careened in a bay in the Malacca Straits. This was done with the knowledge and permission of the local Dutch commandant.

On being relaunched in February 1702, she was wrecked on nearby rocks in the bay. According to an incensed Innes, this was entirely due to *the ignorant, self-willed, and obstinate commander* who had deliberately sent ashore the much more experienced first mate.

Now stranded, they took a house close to the Dutch fort, where the commandant agreed to keep under lock and key their eleven chests of treasure and fine goods. They were unaware that the landlady of their house, the monstrous Mrs Kennedy, was the wife of the Irish pirate. She used her position of trust to slip the ship's young surgeon (and acting second supercargo), Walter Keir, a *philtre* (love potion), the effect of which was to render him utterly besotted with her and unable to refuse her anything. Having got him under her spell, she asked him to steal £1,000 for her. Keir replied that he would readily do so but this would require getting the keys to the treasure boxes from his superior. He was sure that Innes would never consider parting with them.

In her rage she had a local old witch make up a poison which she fed to Keir in his broth. As the young man slipped into a declining state of sweatings and stomach cramps, Captain Campbell and the chief supercargo Innes took passage for China (taking the keys with them) on a passing ship from Surat. They left behind the sickly second supercargo in charge of the remaining stock and in the company of the purser and twelve crewmen.

Not long afterwards, in August 1701, the Scots pirate-chaser and merchant adventurer, Captain Alexander Hamilton, arrived at Malacca. This remarkable man was on his way back to Surat from Siam (Thailand) on his own account when he heard that some fellow Scots were stranded. Concerned for their welfare, he decided to pay them a visit. It is Hamilton who gives us the colourful account of the whole affair.

On arriving at the house, Hamilton found Keir in a *deplorable state* and close to death. Hamilton immediately sent for the fort's physician. The Dutch doctor concluded that the young surgeon had been poisoned but he could do nothing for him until he knew what drug he had ingested. Suspicion immediately fell on Mrs Kennedy, who steadfastly refused to tell him the name of the poison or its source. Hamilton then took charge of affairs and called in an ancient medicine man. For a large fee the medicine man put a hex on the belligerent poisoner. This made her see a demon in her garden that soon had her close to madness and willing to tell the name of her accomplice. The old medicine man then tracked down this witch and threatened her with the same hex. Terrified of him, she promptly told him the nature of the poison she had supplied to Mrs Kennedy. Thereafter, Keir was treated with an antidote and made a good recovery. The evil Mrs Kennedy, however, remained much troubled by her demon.

Captain Hamilton struck a deal with the daily improving young man to return with his ship, after he had fulfilled his trading mission. He would then uplift the *Speedwell*'s crew and cargo and carry them directly back to Scotland. The return of the chief supercargo Innes, however, put paid to this plan, as he would have none of it. He was adamant that he wanted to remain in the East and sell his wares in India.

In his account, Hamilton hints that the reason for Innes's rejection of his rescue plan was the nature of the goods that he had returned with from China: *a Chest of Glassware in their own private Adventure, the most obscenely shameful that I ever saw or heard of among Merchants. There were Priapuses of a large Size, with a scrutom big enough to hold an English pint of liquor.*

So dismissed, Hamilton left Malacca and voyaged on to Surat. Two and a half years later, he came across the chief supercargo at Surat. By then Innes was dying and sought out Hamilton to help settle his affairs and lodge his accounts. From these Hamilton deduced that his attempts to recoup his stock had led to a string of failed trading ventures in Amoy, Bengal and Persia.

Hamilton blamed the complete failure of the *Speedwell* venture on the Company's selection of officers. He described Innes as *a Gentleman of a very courteous Behaviour, and understood a small sword excellently well, but not versed in Merchandize.* Keir, the second supercargo, *was a very good Surgeon, and Master of the French Language, but understood nothing in Accounts.* He kept back his fiercest criticism for the Company's choice of captain, John Campbell. Hamilton had the dubious pleasure of having this master's company on board his own ship for twelve months, during which time he concluded that this Highlander and ex-cattle drover *had a very mean Education, and could not tell what he meant either in speaking or writing. He had a brutal Courage, and was the Husband of three Wives all alive together. He knew nothing either of the Theory or practical Parts of Navigation, and yet had been honoured with a Commission for Lieutenant in the royal navy of England.*

The voyage of the *Speedwell* was not the only Scottish venture that had set out for the East around this time and run into trouble. On 26 May 1701, the Company dispatched to Madagascar two of their Darien veterans, Captain Robert Drummond on the ship *Speedy Return* and Captain John Stewart (or Stuart) on the brig *Content* from 'New' Port Glasgow. Their cargo manifest of: *Brandy, Mum [wheatmeal beer], Strong Beer, Cheese, Knives, Hats, Shoes, Stockings, Chests of firearms and Gunpowder* leaves little doubt as to who their intended customers were – the pirates.

They took little money with them, as they intended to trade for wine at Madeira before rounding the Cape of Good Hope and making for Madagascar. They reached their declared destination without incident by the beginning of May 1702, having touched at Sao Tome and Angola in passage. Once safely in the anchorage of St Mary's Isle, a stream of English and French pirates clambered on board to buy their strong liquors. To earn some additional revenue, Drummond and Stewart agreed to carry a consignment of slaves across to Isle Bourbon (La Réunion), over 300 miles due east. There they sold this human cargo to the local French governor.

While in that island's main harbour, one Captain Honeycomb on the armed East Indiaman *Rook* galley boarded the *Speedy Return*. In high-handed fashion, he quizzed Drummond carefully to ascertain if he was a pirate or an 'interloper' in the trade. On his departure, the Scottish vessels sailed back to Madagascar, arriving in July.

In their quest for new customers, the Scots sailed down the south-east coast to the small anchorage at Maritan, at the mouth of the Matatana River. This was a new settlement raised by the pirate John Bowen (Ap-Owen). He was born in Bermuda to

Welsh parents and, like so many, had turned pirate after suffering great abuse at the hands of his legal masters. Bowen and his men had only recently returned to Madagascar, having wrecked their pirate vessel, the large ex-slaver *Speaker*, on St Thomas Reef, Mauritius, at the end of their raid to the Red Sea.

On their arrival at Maritan, Captain Drummond and his surgeon Andrew Wilkie rowed ashore to a very cordial reception. The officers of the brig *Content*, including Drummond's brother Thomas, also landed and joined in the revelry. According to two eye-witnesses, it was some nine hours after they had gone ashore that a long-boat came alongside the *Speedy Return*. On board was a small party of five armed men led by Bowen, seemingly intent on trading for goods.

Defoe described what followed:

> [on the] pretence of buying some of their Merchandize brought from Europe, and finding a fair Opportunity, the chief Mate, Boatswain, and a Hand or two more only upon the Deck, and the rest at Work in the Hold, they threw off their Mask; each drew out a Pistol and Hanger, and told them, they were all dead Men if they did not retire that Moment to the Cabin. The Surprize was sudden, and they thought it necessary to obey; one of the Pyrates placed himself Centry at the Door, with his Arms in his Hands, and the rest immediately laid the Hatches, and then made a Signal to their Fellows on Shore, as agreed on; upon which, about forty or fifty came on Board, and took quiet Possession of the Ship, and afterwards the Brigantine, without Bloodshed, or striking a stroke.

Some six or eight days later, Bowen and his pirates set sail from Maritan on their newest acquisitions. They left behind stranded the duped Captain Robert Drummond, his chief mate Charles Broudly, the carpenter James Davis and a foremast man John Macclacbee. This was a bitter fate for Scotsmen who had sailed halfway round the world and survived the horrors of Darien. The rest of the Scots crews, numbering around seventy (including the surgeon) were forced.

Bowen made use of their recent intelligence of an encounter with the East Indiaman *Rook*. He decided to set off in pursuit of this potentially valuable prize. This took him back to Isle Bourbon where he found that his quarry had long since gone. He then extended his search to Mauritius, where he found four or five armed ships in the main harbour. Bowen decided not to attack, as they were too strong a force should they decide to stand and fight. He chose instead to return to Madagascar, rounding the southern tip from Fort Dauphin to St Augustine's Bay.

The *Speedy Return* arrived without the *Content*, as the latter had hit a rock-shelf in passage. When the brig eventually appeared a few days later, she was leaking so badly that the decision was taken to abandon her. Her crew was transferred to the *Speedy Return*, after which the *Content* was driven up onshore and burned.

At St Augustine's Bay, they revelled for a fortnight while Bowen considered his next move. This was to seek out and join forces with another group of pirates known to be in the area and sailing under Captain Thomas Howard. The local natives reported that, after taking the East Indiaman *Prosperous* in the bay, they had moved on north to New Mathelage. Sailing up the coast, Bowen found that anchorage empty and so made for the Comoros Islands where he touched at Isle de Johanna. Around Christmas time 1702, he finally caught up with Howard in the anchorage of the neighbouring island of Mayotte.

The two captains made a pact to combine their forces and cruise in company. The following March, they tracked down the

East Indiaman *Pembroke* at anchor and used their long-boats to board her. After plundering her for stores, they forced her carpenter and captain before they let her go with the remainder of her crew.

Captain Wooley was retained to act as their pilot for their planned raid along the Malabar Coast and Red Sea. Soon afterwards, however, the two pirate captains had a disagreement that stalled this plan for several months. It was not until midsummer that they set aside their differences and reunited at Johanna before setting off for the Red Sea.

Contrary winds put paid to this plan and they found themselves off the Indian coast near Surat. Around the end of August the quest for rich prizes met with success, as they sighted a small convoy of four large Moorish vessels out from Surat heading for Mocha. During the chase these four vessels split into pairs, one pair sailing north while the other pair ran south along the coast. The *Speedy Return* pursued the latter group and eventually came up with and took the largest. Bowen took this prize back to their rendezvous at Rajapore where Howard soon joined him. Howard had caught and looted one of his victims, which brought their combined booty to £70,000 – a princely sum.

At Rajapore they decided to burn the *Prosperous* and the *Speedy Return* after transferring their men and armaments to Bowen's great Moorish prize (700 tons). He renamed her the *Defiance*, which, with fifty-six cannons and manned by around 160 lascars and around 100 fighting pirates, was now a formidable warship. During the refit, the very ill Captain Wooley was finally allowed to go ashore. Bowen and Howard then set off on a cruise down the Malabar Coast where they took and looted the unfortunate *Pembroke* for a second time.

By now Bowen had had enough and sailed back to Mauritius where the company disbanded. Howard and his men took over the *Defiance* and went off on their own account, while Bowen and forty of his men headed for retirement. In Bowen's case, this proved short-lived as he died from an intestinal complaint within six months.

It was during the *Defiance*'s stay at Mauritius that two of the forced men from Drummond's *Speedy Return* made their bid for freedom. The eldest, the 38-year-old Peter Freeland of Slains, near Aberdeen, escaped, taking with him the 21-year-old Israel Phipenny (or Fisonne) from New Salem. Phipenny had been an apprentice to the Glasgow merchant George Lockhart before joining the crew of the *Speedy Return* at Port Glasgow.

After the pirates had gone their separate ways, these two men managed to secure a berth on a passing homeward-bound East Indiaman, the *Raper* galley of London, that landed them at Portsmouth at the end of March 1705. It was close to four years since they had left the Clyde.

Waiting to meet them was John Green, whose brother Captain Thomas Green was currently languishing in Edinburgh Castle vaults awaiting execution for the *Piracy & Robbery* of the *Speedy Return* and the *Murder* of her entire crew. His hanging was scheduled to take place in twelve days' time, having already had an eight-day stay of execution due to the direct intervention of the Queen.

John Green rushed these two walking ghosts before the Mayor of Portsmouth, who took their sworn affidavits as to the true fate of the *Speedy Return* and her men – taken by Madagascan pirates without a shot fired or a drop of Scottish blood spilled.

CHAPTER 10

The Piracy Trial of Captain Green

The affidavits of the *Speedy Return*'s two crewmen, Freeland and Phipenny, taken at Portsmouth were immediately sent by express to London. There they were eventually brought before Robert Harley, the Secretary of State for the 'Northern Department'. Such was the significance of their testimony to Anglo-Scottish affairs that he had a copy of them forwarded to Edinburgh. These were accompanied by a plea from Queen Anne for a further stay of execution for the crew of the *Worcester*, whilst their case was fully reviewed. By now eight days had passed since the taking of the original depositions.

The messenger duly arrived in Edinburgh on the morning of 11 April 1705, three hours before the scheduled execution on Leith Sands of the first batch of condemned pirates: Captain Thomas Green; his chief mate, John Madder; and the gunner, John Simpson.

The trial of Green and the crew of the *Worcester* in Edinburgh had, for months, provided a focus and outlet for the seething resentment against England that had been fomenting in the Queen's Northern Kingdom for over a decade. The inevitable underlying resentment of a more powerful neighbour had been exacerbated since the news reached Scotland of the callous treatment meted out by the English governors of the Caribbean islands and American colonies to the sick and the dying survivors fleeing from the ill-fated Darien venture. These officials, it must be said, were acting under a direct Royal proclamation from King William to turn the Scots colonists away. As a result, of the thousands of men and women who perished in this forlorn venture, many hundreds – *who lookt rather like skelets than men, being starved* – died needlessly.

The suffering of the Darien survivors continued long afterwards. Captain Pincarton and his crew of the *Dolphin*, captured by the Spanish, had been conveyed in chains to Seville. As their Scots Company's commission was not recognised by William, the Spaniards felt well within their rights to try them as pirates. It took nineteen months of delicate negotiations to secure their release, during which a number had died in captivity. The overall outcome was that there was hardly a Lowland Scots seafaring family or noted house that had not lost a relative at Darien or in the retreat – not to mention the squandering of a quarter of the nation's available wealth and an unbearable loss of national pride.

Even before Scotland's colonial aspirations finally sank with the Company's two great ships – the *Rising Sun* and the *Duke of Hamilton* – at Charleston, high-handed English naval commanders in Scottish waters were making a mockery of Scotland's supposed independent sovereignty. English navy captains, such as Pottinger on HMS *Dartmouth*, while defending the realm from the Jacobite threat, took to intercepting Scottish ships returning from the Americas in breach of the English Navigation Acts and carried them off south as prize. These acts were done in blatant disregard of the Scottish Admiralty. The Scottish Privy Council had fervently pleaded with Queen Mary, in William's absence abroad, to reprimand these officers and have the seized vessels returned – but to no avail. Much was blamed on the thinly disguised conspiracy between the English Establishment and Royal Companies to do all in their power, short of open war at sea, to block Scotland's attempts to break into the world's markets.

It is indicative of the national mood that the first act of the reconvened Scottish Parliament of January 1700 was to display its enormous displeasure at the critics of the Darien Scheme. They ordered that a copy of a 'treasonable' pamphlet then circulating, entitled *A defence of the Scots abdicating Darien* by 'Britanno sed Dunensi', should be publicly burned by the city hangman. Thereafter, the Lords of the Scottish Treasury offered a reward of £500 for the arrest of the alleged author, the turncoat Walter Herries.

At the same time a motion, calling on King William to censure the English Parliament for *intermeddling in the affairs of this kingdom, and the invasion of the sovereignty and independence of our King and Parliament*, was narrowly defeated. Two Edinburgh engravers who dared to lampoon the divisions in a political cartoon, were arrested and charged with 'lease making'. This ancient term for slander was normally reserved for insulting a royal minister and so carried the death penalty. On this occasion, however, the jury had the eminent good sense to find that this petty crime did not warrant such a serious charge or punishment and so dismissed the case as 'not proven'.

The death of the heir, Prince William, the last of Anne's thirteen children, during that year threw open the whole question of the Succession. The English Parliament passed the Act of Settlement that handed the English crown to the Hanoverian descendants of James I (VI of Scotland) on Anne's death. The Scottish Parliament seized on this opportunity and passed their own Act of Security in 1704. This threatened to choose a different successor for the Scottish throne, thereby ending the Union of the Crowns of 1603, unless the 'freedom of trade' issue was resolved in their favour.

This tidal wave of ill-feeling in the North might have subsided without bloodletting, had not the *Annandale* incident reignited the nation's hatred of their overbearing neighbour. As the schism descended into a 'tit-for-tat' spiral of hostile legislation, the Company of Scotland, bereft of vessels, bought the majority share of an armed London merchantman of 220 tons and 20 guns in October 1703. Her previous owners were a small group of independent English merchants led by John Johnson – an Englishman, or said to be – who had yet to purchase a licence from the English East India Company for her intended voyage to the East as an independent trader.

Her new Scots owners renamed her the *Annandale*, in honour of the Company's London Director, the Marquis of Annandale, and sent their agent, Robert Laurie, from Edinburgh to oversee her fitting-out while still in the Thames. Her mission was, ostensibly, to retrieve the valuable cargo of the *Speedwell* wrecked in the Malacca Straits. The Company also bought a three-quarters' share in her outgoing cargo that included £2,500 in Mexican silver dollars.

To legitimise the *Annandale*'s passage 'East of the Cape of Good Hope', the Scots Company sent to London copies of their 'Letters Patent' (granted by an Act of the Scottish

Parliament) and a 'Letter of Marque' signed by the Earl of Queensferry (the Queen's Commissioner for Scotland). The latter gave her the status of privateer, empowered to capture any French and Spanish vessels she might encounter. These documents were given to her commander, John Ap-Rice, who had previously been a part-owner and was now retained as her captain. After a suspiciously long delay getting clearance from the Customs House of London, during time which her papers were subjected to *a stricter manner than was ever practised on any foreigners*, she sailed down-river to Gravesend.

While she was moored there, the London-based agents of the Company of Scotland, Captain Alexander Gawne and William Murray, found out that their newly appointed captain was a common debtor and a *rogue* of the first order, who had purloined her bill of sale. They deduced that his intention was to make off with the *Annandale* and her cargo at the first opportunity.

Without clear proof of ownership and in a hostile environment, they sent an urgent dispatch to Laurie (now serving on board as the second supercargo) that Ap-Rice was to be turned out of his command and never allowed to set foot on her again. Ap-Rice however, proved highly obstructive to his dismissal and demanded £100 in compensation for loss of earnings. This was refused and he was forcibly removed, after three days' belligerence, with only his 'river wages'.

On landing ashore he made straight for the offices of the East India Company. There he divulged his insider information as to the designs of the interloping Scots. They immediately supported his personal claim for compensation (which had now increased to £20,000) through the Court of Chancery and applied for a warrant to stop her sailing on his behalf.

Back on board the *Annandale*, the senior supercargo, Mallory Peirson, was ordered to take command, abort the voyage to the East Indies and immediately bring her to the safety of Scottish waters. Common sense, however, dictated that Peirson should wait for a convoy (it was wartime) to escort his ship through the English Channel before making for the Clyde. It was, therefore, not until late January 1704 that the *Annandale* finally got under way.

A few days later, on 1 February, while riding to her anchors at the Downs, off the south coast of England, she was boarded by customs officers under the pretence of looking for stolen money. They were led by the Tide Surveyor for London, Charles Robertson, who was accompanied by an armed naval party from HMS *Dunwich*. The Lieutenant in charge promptly pressed twenty-one of the *Scots Dogs* he found on board the *Annandale* and had them rowed over to his warship. Laurie (the second supercargo) later reported to his directors in Edinburgh that those Scots seamen remaining on board were then subjected to great abuse, their captors *threatening to put them in Irons, drawing their Cutlasses, cocking their Muskets at them, and Swearing they'd shoot them through the Heads, as if they had been Robbers and Pirates.*

All this brought vehement protests from the *Annandale*'s officers. They produced Queensferry's Royal Commission as proof of their right to proceed unmolested. To this Robertson scornfully replied *that he valued it not a Pin, for that he had the East Indies Company's Warrant to Indemnify him, and that they had a long purse to defend themselves in Westminster Hall.*

So saying, he had all the locks broken and sent his men to rummage the cargo and cabins. When he eventually departed, he took with him the ship's officers, their papers and the treasure chests. He left behind his junior officer, Russell Catcliffe, with a gang of ruffians hired by the English Company. Having little control over these men, Catcliffe could not stop them looting the few remaining Scots crewmen of their personal possessions. While engaged in this malicious act, they taunted Laurie with the boast that their Company had *given Orders, [to] take care to find Mr Innes, Supercargo of the* Speedwell *in the East Indies, and make sure of [seizing his] effects.*

At one stage they ran the *Annandale* aground. After she was refloated, she was carried into Dover where her general cargo was landed and her sails and yards stripped from her masts. There she lay while the matter of her ownership was contested in the courts.

As Robertson had predicted, it was a costly affair. The directors of the Company of Scotland, on hearing of her seizure and the outrageous treatment of their officers and men, dispatched their secretary, Roderick McKenzie, directly to the Queen with a petition. She heard the Scots Company's list of grievances in a session of the Privy Council, at which the Attorney and Solicitors-General were present. During this meeting she expressed her sympathy for the Scots' cause but heeded her councillors' advice and refused to intervene directly. Her pronouncement was, therefore, that this highly contentious affair was a matter for the English courts to settle.

In the run-up to this politically explosive hearing, the English company directors put it about that they were prepared to spend £100,000 on legal costs, rather than release the *Annandale*. This precedent-making threat had the desired effect of deterring other would-be speculators from taking up a similar commission with the Company of Scotland. Only the previous month, James, Earl of Morton, had signed Articles of Agreement with the directors to send out his small well-armed vessel, the *Morton*, to the East Indies. Still in the Thames, she was within immediate reach of the agents of the English Companies and so he prudently cancelled her departure. A similar scheme to fit out the *Hannah* galley on behalf of the Company of Scotland, by the London merchant Ainsworth, was also dropped; even though she lay out of harm's way at Burntisland in the Firth of Forth.

After a false start, the 'trial' of the *Annandale* was finally called before the Bar of the Court of Exchequer on 28 June 1704. The 'charge' was that the *Annandale* was intending to trade 'East of the Cape of Good Hope' without licence from the English Company, whose monopoly was enshrined in an English Act of Parliament. The vessel and her cargo should, therefore, be condemned as the prize to the Company.

Many of the English directors were present on the day and their cause was presented by a battery of nine eminent Queen's Counsel. Much to the exasperation of the Scots Company lawyers, the Attorney and Solicitors-General, who had recently advised the Queen on the matter, were amongst their number.

The atmosphere in the courtroom changed to utter disbelief when Captain John Ap-Rice was presented as a legal witness for the English Company's cause. Remonstrate all they might against the appearance of this man – *known for his notorious Treachery, avow'd Malice and evil Reputation* – the judges dismissed the Scots Company lawyers' objections and Ap-Rice was allowed to testify as to the designs of the interloping Scots.

The Scots defence was straightforward. The *Annandale* was the legal property of the Company of Scotland, whose charter was enshrined in an Act of the Scottish Parliament. As such, she had every right to go about their business in English waters without fear of seizure of their vessels by the English Company. In fact, she should be shown the same respect as vessels of the Dutch East India Company in similar circumstances. In any case, the *Annandale* was not heading out on a passage to the East Indies but on a coastal passage to the Clyde.

After ten hours of legal debate, the four Barons of the Exchequer gave down their verdict: three to one in favour of the English Company claim. The *Annandale* and her cargo were duly condemned as lawful prize to the English East India Company.

The following day, 4 July, the legal counsel for the Scots Company moved for an 'Arrestment of the Judgement'. As this was the last day sitting for this Court before the summer recess, the lawyers for the English Company had no difficulty in having this appeal put back to the autumn. In the meantime, the *Annandale* was released back to her Scots owners, on their finding security for her value and that of her cargo.

Before she could be refitted to sail from Dover, Ap-Rice struck again. No doubt with prompting from his new backers, he had his agent nail an Admiralty 'Process of Arrest' at the foot of her mainmast. This was for £3,000 damages he claimed he had suffered as a result of the legal action. The Scots agents in London were, yet again, forced to find security for this sum before the *Annandale* could be taken back round to Deptford in the Thames.

She had only just arrived there when the opportunity for reprisal presented itself in Scottish waters on 28 July. This was when the English East Indiaman, the *Worcester* (180 tons, 16 guns and 32 men), put into the Firth of Forth.

She was a private small trader with the second-rank English 'Two Million Company' (operating under an East India Company licence) on her home run to London after an absence of two years. She had rounded Scotland, in company with sixteen Dutch and two English East Indiamen, to avoid capture by the large French privateers that stalked the English Channel. Once clear of the Pentland Firth, however, the three London-bound Indiamen had left the convoy and turned south.

Sailing down the east coast of Scotland, the slow and leaky *Worcester* soon fell behind the other two vessels. Left by herself and with her gunpowder casks wet, her captain, Thomas Green, concluded that his ship was now highly vulnerable to attack from the small French and Jacobite privateers that worked close inshore. He decided, therefore, to call into Fraserburgh, on 19 July, to buy replacement gunpowder.

There he sent a lengthy letter, via Edinburgh, to his London owners detailing his voyage and his intention to put into Leith to repair the leak and await the next convoy for Newcastle. To this end, he loaded a few casks of new dry gunpowder and took on a Scottish pilot.

Had the *Worcester* been a large 'regular berth' of the East India Company (that is, carrying naval-rated heavy armament and three times as many men) it is doubtful whether the agents of the Company of Scotland could have secured her in compensation for the *Annandale* without an immediate fight or expectation of retaliation. As it was, she was a perfect target and her presence in Scottish waters was already known in Edinburgh. To prepare the political ground for her seizure, the directors of the Company of Scotland presented a petition to the Marquis of Tweeddale – the Queen's High Commissioner to the Scottish

Parliament. In it, they graphically portrayed the violence and insults of the *Annandale* incident. These were presented as but the latest in a series of *repeated Acts of Violence and Oppression* committed against their legitimate interests. Such blatant, state-approved, English aggression demanded retaliation in kind.

The following day, 12 August, two weeks after her arrival, the *Worcester* was seized by a simple deception. The now Anglophobic Secretary of the Company, Roderick McKenzie, armed with an arrest warrant, rowed over to her as she lay to her anchor off Burntisland. He had with him a small number of men and bottles of wine and brandy. Coming alongside, he hailed the watch and offered to make merry in exchange for a tour of this fine vessel that had come all the way from India.

In the absence of the captain and senior officers, the un-suspecting crewmen invited them aboard and ushered them into the great cabin. The rest of the crew (at least six of whom were Scots) joined them in a bowl of punch, suitably laced with McKenzie's brandy.

As the wine flowed freely, McKenzie requested that they strike up a hearty song. The *Worcester*'s boatswain, James Burn, later testified as to what happened:

> *whilst we were in our mirth, a Scots Man-of-War, then at anchor in Leith Road, near us, fired a Gun with Shot, immediately after which the said Mr McKenzie rose up, and told us, we had been very kind and civil to him, and he would now sing us a Song; but not being used to sing[ing], he had his Song in Writing, and drew out a piece of paper, and told us it was a Warrant from the Africa and East India Company of Scotland to seize our ship for Reprisal for the* Annandale *seized in England, or words to that effect. On which all the Scots in the great Cabin drew their swords, and said, we all were their prisoners.*

The warship that signalled the seizure was the sixth-rater *Royal Mary* of the 'Old Scots Navy', under the command of the closet Jacobite, Commodore Thomas Gordon. He had previously used his Royal Commission as a naval officer to aid and abet the Company of Scotland. His signal was probably to tell McKenzie that Captain Green and his officers, who were in Edinburgh at the time, had been safely detained. Firing a cannonball, rather than just a blank powder charge, also served to intimidate the *Worcester's* crew at the critical moment of seizure. It can also be assumed that Gordon had the *Royal Mary* standing close guard in the Forth in case the East Indiamen, that had recently parted company from her, came to her aid.

After the *Worcester* was securely in the hands of the Company's agents, she was placed under the supervision of Captain David Munro. He decided to minimise the risk of an attempt by her crew to retake her, by turning the ordinary seamen ashore. They were evicted without their two years' pay and left to fend for themselves as best they could. A few made their way to Leith, while most had the good sense to head straight for the border and London.

After the seizure, the young Captain Green and his Scots-born first mate, John Madder, were given their freedom to take up lodgings with Mrs Barclay (or Barlett) in Edinburgh, whilst the fate of their vessel was decided.

It was Munro who first reported an undertow of unease and tensions amongst the five crewmen retained on board to maintain the *Worcester*. The first incident he noted was when he was stopped and questioned by the gunner, James Simpson, as he passed by his hammock. This restless sailor was very anxious to know if there was another reason for the seizure of the *Worcester* – one that might imperil his life?

A day or two later, Munro overheard a heated exchange between the overwrought ship's carpenter, Henry Keigle, and the gunner's mate, Andrew Robison, as to their non-payment of wages. Keigle was for both of them abandoning their posts on the *Worcester* and going ashore. But Robison had already decided to *take his Hazard and stick with the ship while there [was] any hope.*

These incidents would have been dismissed as their due concern for their predicament, had not Robison retorted to the carpenter's continuing complaints: *this is just Judgment of God on us, for the Wickedness committed in our last Voyage; and I'm afraid it will pursue us further, since that, being reduced to so small a Number aboard, for if five of us cannot agree amongst ourselves.* Months later, in the witness box, Munro, rather theatrically, placed great emphasis on the fact that Robison had uttered his remark *after a heavy Groan or two.*

Matters took a turn for the worse when the *Worcester* was moved into the heads of Burntisland harbour and stripped of her sails and yards. In doing so, she was immobilised and could no longer be sailed away by a 'cutting out' party sent in by the English East India Company or the English Navy. For the five-man watch on board, this indicated that their ship was not going to be released in the foreseeable future.

Soon afterwards, her dejected anchor-watch adjourned to the great cabin to drown their sorrows in a bowl of punch. It was during this heavy drinking session that one of the Company's guards boasted about the daring exploits of Commodore Gordon when chasing Jacobite and French raiders. Not to be outdone, the tipsy ship's steward, George Haines, bawled out: *our sloop was more terrible upon the coast of Malabar, than ever Captain Gordon was or will be to the French Privateers on the Coast of Scotland; For a better Sailer than that sloop never carried canvas!* He was referring to a small sloop that the *Worcester* had carried dismantled in her hull, and had reassembled at Delagoa Bay in Southern Mozambique to act as the inshore coastal trader while in the Indian Ocean.

Having raised the image of the East, the 'Gentlemen of the Scots Company' present in the great cabin enquired of Haines (by now *lukewarm with punch*) if he had met the overdue *Speedy Return* and *Content* on his travels. He answered that he had heard of them but not seen them. He then merrily volunteered: *it's no great Matter, you need not trouble yourself about them, for I believe you will not see them in haste.* This fateful remark instantly aroused their keenest interest. They pressed him on what might be the reason for his comment. At this point Haines, despite becoming aware of the sudden change in tone of the conversation, blurted out that he had heard: *that they were turned pirates, and that one of them had eight guns and the other Twelve or Fourteen, to the best of his memory.*

Haines was not only a drunken braggart but also a womaniser. He soon had romantic designs on the young women from Burntisland who often visited the ship in harbour. During the following weeks, one nineteen-year-old lass, Anne Seaton, appeared to return his advances. What Haines was not aware of was that this 'femme fatale' had a sweetheart on board the missing *Speedy Return*. The three other crewmen then on board, Simpson, Keigle and Robison, listened with increasing despair as Haines regaled this young lady with swaggering tales. At the first opportunity they took him aside and severely threatened him if he did not put a stop to his loose and inventive tongue.

Such was their concern that two of the English crewmen who had been turned ashore, George Kitchen and Thomas Whitehead, were recruited to spirit Haines away before he could do any more mischief. The plan was for all three to take horse to the neighbouring town of Kinghorn, further along the coast, where a ferry regularly crossed to the busy seaport of Leith. Once there, a berth could easily be had on one of the fast sailing smacks that ran as packets to London.

They were, apparently, unaware that Haines was being watched. For, as they mounted their hired horses, they were intercepted by a posse of local men led by George Ker. The steward was subsequently delivered unceremoniously back on board the *Worcester*, where his fellow crewmen ensured that he remained muzzled.

To circumnavigate his vigilant minders, his temptress – Miss Seaton – arranged for him to visit her at her mother's house in Burntisland. There he was plied with drink and engaged in probing conversations in front of witnesses. During one of his performances, in September, the drunken Haines fell into a fit of melancholia in the presence of John Henderson, Writer to the Signet, and William Wood, a gunner with the Royal Artillery. When asked what was troubling him he wrung his hands and melodramatically replied: *It is a wonder that since we did not sink at Sea, that God does not make the Ground open up and swallow us up when we came ashore, for the Wickedness, that has been committed during the last voyage on board that old Bitch Bess.* And he turned and pointed to the *Worcester* riding in the harbour.

Later, while walking with Haines along Burntisland Links, the gunner Wood opened a conversation about a relative of the

Worcester's chief mate. The rumour was, he recalled, that Madder's uncle had been burned alive in oil at Amsterdam for attempted arson on vessels in that port. Haines duly obliged him with the retort: *that if what Captain Madder had done during this last Voyage were as well known, he deserved as much as his Uncle met with!*

The following month, while Haines, with one of the ship's two 'black' servants in attendance, was enjoying a toast or two in the Widow Seaton's house, he was confronted by James Wilkie. James was the brother of Andrew, the surgeon on the *Speedy Return*, and was accompanied by his anxious mother. Cornered by their questions as to the fate of the *Speedy Return*, Haines *fell into a passion and screamed: Damn me, what have I to do with Captain Drummond?*

It took some time and a few more cups of punch to restore his humour, after which, he was persuaded to return to the subject. He eventually divulged that, while they were on the Malabar Coast, a passing Dutch ship had informed them that Drummond had turned pirate, whereupon Captain Green had ordered the *Worcester*'s sloop, christened the *Delagoa* by the crew, to be made ready in case they were attacked. Fortunately for them, the Scots pirate never made an appearance.

Perhaps to retain the attention of his wearying audience, he added a tantalising aside that, at the time of the seizure of the *Worcester* in the Forth, *he had in his custody, that which he would not have fallen into the Seizers Hands for twice the value of the ship!* When queried as to what this mysterious item might be, he curtly replied that he had long since thrown it overboard, declaring as he did so: *let them seek it now at the Bottom of the Sea!*

James Wilkie tried steering him back to his dark secret by enquiring about the value of the *Worcester*. The braggart in Haines rose to the bait, for he chose to disclose that she was not as rich as would be expected after her two-year voyage; but there were *things still hidden in her* that had escaped detection at the first rummage by the agents of the company. Things of which he, of course, knew the exact whereabouts and which could only otherwise be found by stripping her hull *board from board*.

Mrs Wilkie, by now deeply distressed by Haines's evasive ranting, left the room with the Widow Seaton. Out of his earshot, Mrs Wilkie pleaded with the Widow to make him tell her what he knew of her son. The Widow counselled her that, as he was a suitor for her daughter's hand, Anne was the person best positioned to pry open his secrets. This was agreed and the Wilkies took their leave. Some time later, the conceited Haines confided to his attentive belle that *he found they had a design to pump him, but that they should not be the wiser of him, tho[ugh] what he had said, he had said*. At which point Anne decided that the game had run its course.

The following morning she left Burntisland and made for the house of Kenneth McKenzie in the Canongate, Edinburgh. He was a kinsman of the secretary and himself an agent of the company. He listened with the deepest interest as she divulged all she had heard and what she suspected. Spurred to action by her rendition of Haines's boast of 'things' hidden in the *Worcester*, he went straight to the Committee in Council of the company.

They immediately ordered a more thorough search of the *Worcester*. At the same time they set in motion enquiries with a view to raising a case against Captain Green and his crew for piracy of the *Speedy Return* and the murder of her crew.

The further rummage was exhaustive but revealed nothing directly incriminating. The searchers did, however, report to the Committee that they had found the nature of the ship's books and the state of the cargo highly suspicious. Some of her ledgers were written in a cipher, which they held to be circumstantial evidence of some kind of clandestine activity, not befitting an honest trader. Furthermore, her cargo was in a dishevelled state, with a number of bales and chests unmarked. This state of affairs, they maintained, would never have been allowed by a self-respecting supercargo. Both observations raised the question: was this plundered cargo that had been dumped in the hold?

The investigation had, by now, gained its own momentum. The inquisitors moved forward on the assumption that, as pirates, they would have taken an oath of secrecy. Unless one could be made to confess, others had to be found who could testify to their guilt. Their search for witnesses quickly led them to the two 'black' servants still on board the *Worcester*: Antonio Ferdinando, the cook's mate, and Antonio Francisco, manservant to Captain Green.

In Ferdinando they found what they were looking for – the vital eye-witness to an act of piracy and murder. He was a Portuguese-speaking Indian and told them, through an interpreter, of a terrible act that took place at sea. This event happened off the coast of Malabar, between Calicut and Tellicherry, in January or February 1703.

According to him, the *Worcester* had come up with another vessel flying the same flag and Captain Green, the supercargo (now deceased) and the purser went aboard her. On their return the Captain ordered the sloop to be made ready to attack the other vessel. The sloop was then armed with four cannons and two swivel-guns. Madder was put in charge of the twenty men, including Ferdinando, who manned the *Delagoa* sloop for the assault.

The sloop, being a fine sailer, caught up with the other vessel and engaged her in a fire-fight over two successive days, but did not have the weight of shot to overpower her. On the third day, the *Worcester* finally came up and fired her heavier cannon. Whereupon, Madder then led a boarding party which took the vessel. They then proceeded to brutally murder the captured crew with hatchets and throw their bodies overboard. Ferdinando reckoned that ten men died in this manner. During the engagement he was one of a number of the *Worcester's* crew who received a wound, the scar of which he still bore.

Afterwards, some of the captured vessel's cargo was taken aboard the *Worcester*. The prize was then sailed to the Keilon River where she was sold to Coge Commodo, a native merchant and servant of the local king.

This hair-raising story appeared to be corroborated by the testimony of the *Worcester's* 26-year-old surgeon, Charles May, now residing in Edinburgh. At the time of the alleged piratical attack, he was ashore with one of the seamen, John Reynolds. Even so, he claimed that he had heard and seen much.

In his statement he related that, as he stood at a landing-place four miles from Callicoilean, he heard cannon-fire far out to sea. Later that day, when he was in the company of Coge Commodo and the *Worcester's* 'linguister', Francisco de Olivera, he enquired what caused the shooting. He was told that *the* Worcester *had gone out and was Fighting at Sea with another Ship.*

Early the next morning, he was back at the landing-place and saw that the *Worcester* had returned to her anchorage, some four miles offshore. Near her stern there appeared to be riding another vessel. Later that morning, the *Worcester's* long-boat came in over the sand bar, despite a heavy running sea. The surgeon asked what was the emergency that warranted such a risk. He was told that Madder had sent them to get a 'Pinguetta' (native boat) to bring water out to the *Worcester* as they *had spilt and staved all their Water Aboard*. The men looked exhausted. They explained away their fatigue on having been *busking* all night. The surgeon took this to be a sailor's term for working a vessel back upwind to her mooring after having been driven from her anchors by adverse conditions. The prosecution would, however, later claim that this term was pirate parlance for fitting-out a merchant vessel as a fighting raider.

Five or six days passed before the surgeon, carrying his new supply of medicines, went back on board the *Worcester*. He was immediately struck by the shambles of bales and chests on the deck and asked Madder, *what have you got there, you are full of Business?* His enquiry was met with a curse and a command to *go mind his Plaister Box*. Soon afterwards Ferdinando presented himself to the surgeon with a bandaged arm that proved to be fractured and gashed. When asked who had applied the dressing, the Indian said a Dutch doctor at Cochin, a port further up the coast. Two other crewmen, Duncan Mackay and Edward Cumming, also needed his skills for injuries. At the time he thought these wounds could have been the result of a fight, but he could not be certain.

The other servant, Francisco, was a Portuguese-speaking African manservant, bought by Captain Green at Delagoa Bay while trading for ivory. He proved to be of little use to the inquisitors as he had been chained in the hold most of the time of the alleged act of piracy. In fact, he only knew what Ferdinando had told him of the incident.

Some time later, a Leith goldsmith and seal-maker, John Glen, came forward to the Committee with new and damning information. He said that, a few days after the *Worcester* arrived at Burntisland, the first mate Madder had taken him aside. Once in the privacy of the great cabin, Madder had shown him a seal that he had in his possession. Glen described it as mounted on a lignum vitae handle and bearing the unmistakable coat-of-arms of the Company of Scotland: *the St Andrew's Cross, a Dromedarie or Camel with a Castle on the back of it, a ship with a Rising Sun above the Helmet, and two wild Men as Supporters … near the bigness of an English Half-Crown.* To the interviewing Committee this was an indisputable piece of hard evidence as to what Haines had hinted was hidden in the *Worcester*. Indeed, this sighting of their seal proved to the Council that there was a direct link between the act of piracy reported by Ferdinando and at least one of the missing Scots vessels.

The Committee duly handed over their findings to the Prosecutor for the High Court of Admiralty of Scotland. On 15 December 1704, Green and Madder were arrested at their lodgings in Edinburgh on the charge of piracy, robbery and murder. At the same time, the five crewmen on the *Worcester* and seven others found in the immediate area of Burntisland and Leith were rounded up.

They were marched off to four separate locations: Edinburgh Castle, the Old Town Tolbooth (close to St Giles on the Royal Mile), the Canongate Tolbooth (further down the Mile), and Leith Tolbooth. The star witnesses for the prosecution, Ferdinando, May and Francisco, were also detained in the Castle, although they were given their liberty within its walls.

By now Edinburgh was in uproar, even though the Prosecutor's final charges were careful to state that the alleged heinous crimes were perpetrated against an unknown ship, manned by an unidentified English-speaking crew. Indeed, the indictment did not mention at any time (or in any place) Captain Drummond, or any member of his crew, or the *Speedy Return*.

It may have been a coincidence, though highly unlikely, that around the time of their arrest, the Lord High Admiral of England formally sanctioned the seizure of the *Annandale*. This decision meant that henceforth all Scottish vessels found trading in breach of any of the English Companies' monopolies were legal prize.

The stalemate was complete. It was now no longer possible for the company vessels of one nation to survive unmolested in the sovereign waters of the other.

The trial of Captain Green and his crew commenced on 4 March 1705. Sitting on the bench were two regular judges, James Graham and Robert Forbes. Such was the gravity of the offences and the political overtones of the case that they were joined by the Earl of Loudoun, the Earl of Belhaven, Robert Dundas (Senior) of Arniston, John Home of Blackadder and John Cockburn of Ormiston.

The prosecution team of eight advocates was led by Alexander Higgins, the Procurator Fiscal for the Admiralty Court. The defence team of six advocates was led by Sir David Theirs. The jury was hand-picked from the most interested parties – five sea captains (led by Archibald Drummond of Leith) and ten Edinburgh merchants. Most of these jurors had close connections with the Company of Scotland.

The defence, predictably, opened the hearing with a legal challenge as to the Court's competence to adjudicate a case brought against an English master and an English vessel for supposed crimes committed thousands of miles away. This argument was set aside as the Court deemed itself empowered by the Law of Nations to deal with any act of piracy committed in international waters.

The defence then followed up with a formal request that Captain Green should be tried first, as the rest of the accused were seamen doing his bidding. They stated that, like the late Captain William Kidd, Green held a quasi-naval commission to suppress piracy in the Indian Ocean (as granted by the late King William, under the Great Seal). Failing that, those crewmen standing in the dock who were plainly innocent (notably the second mate, John Reynolds, who had been ashore at the time of the alleged attack) should be freed so that they could bear witness for the defence. Both these motions were denied. The judges ruled that the captain and his crew were *socii criminis* (common criminals) and not acting in any naval capacity that might excuse an attack on another vessel.

With all procedural points of law dealt with, the two-week trial of all fifteen defendants got under way with the interrogation of the only eye-witness to the crime, Ferdinando. This examination was conducted with the help of Captain George Yeaman of Dundee as interpreter.

Given the deeply held prejudices of the day towards 'black' people, Higgins first took time and care to build the credibility of Ferdinando with the jury. He stated that the 24-year-old Indian was a baptised Christian and the son of Christian parents. As such, he fully understood the gravity of the oath he had taken as witness. He also pointed out that Ferdinando had joined the *Worcester* at Anjango on the Malabar Coast, only a few days before the alleged act of piracy. He had, therefore, little time or occasion to nurture such a strong grievance against this captain and his crew that he should perjure himself in an act of malice.

Ferdinando was then invited to relate the story of his involve-ment in a terrible act of piracy to the jury. This evidence was seemingly verified by May and Francisco. Higgins then proceeded to underpin his case with the witnesses to Haines's rantings at Burntisland. The seal which Madder had shown the Leith master had, unfortunately, since gone missing, so a lookalike was displayed for the benefit of the jury.

The defence opened with a pre-emptive broadside on the flimsiness of the charges, which never specified the exact time or place of the crimes or the identity of the victims. How, Sir David Theirs demanded, could these men in the *pannel* ever prove their innocence if these essential details were not forthcoming? Prophetically, he put it to the jury that the vessel and crew alluded to might well have been shipwrecked or taken by pirates elsewhere. Witnesses to these events may have survived and so be able to provide alibis – if only the vessel was identified in the charge. After all, this vessel had not been sunk, but sold to others who would have knowledge of its identity and ultimate fate.

He declared that any verdict of 'proven' returned on such vague charges could never be safe. In support of his argument, he cited the opinions of the ancient criminologist Pharinacius and the great Scots jurist, Sir George McKenzie. The prosecution had, he claimed, ignored the most basic rules of evidence, as laid down by the Constitution of the Roman Emperor Theodosius.

The defence laid great emphasis on the fact that a number of accused had had the opportunity to escape. They had chosen not to, even though they were well aware of the rumours of piracy that surrounded their vessel. Indeed, one of the ordinary seaman, John Bannantine, a native of Scotland, had presented himself at the Canongate Tolbooth after the arrest of the others, intent on clearing his name. This was not, the defence proclaimed, the action of a guilty man. These arguments failed in their objective, namely, to have the case dismissed before moving to a formal defence.

Forced to proceed, the central plank of the defence strategy was to discredit the testimonies of the two main prosecution witnesses, Ferdinando and May, as riddled with inconsistencies. The principal discrepancy was that Ferdinando had stated that the piratical attack took place over a period of three days. The surgeon, on the other hand, was adamant that the *Worcester* had been gone only one night from her mooring.

Furthermore, the cook's mate stated that the location of the alleged act of piracy was well over a hundred miles from the shore where May heard gunfire. This could not be possible as the lead-sheathed *Worcester* was a slow sailer and could never have been in all the places mentioned by Ferdinando in the time-scale given. If Ferdinando's story of a sea-fight was true, the defence demanded, why were there no marks of cannon-shot to be seen on the *Worcester's* hull?

Pressing home their argument, the defence pointed to the obvious fact that there had not been one word of a piratical attack along the Malabar Coast during the time of the alleged incident. Such news invariably spread like wildfire along the Indian Coast and would have been reported back to London by now. Indeed, at least two East Indiamen had docked recently – those that had accompanied the *Worcester* on her homeward passage – carrying the most recent intelligence of events on the Malabar Coast. The inescapable conclusion was that the *Worcester* had never been involved in an act of piracy. Ferdinando, for reasons known only to himself, was lying.

As for the surgeon's circumstantial evidence of hearing gunfire, the jury were informed that there was another, more plausible, explanation – *shooting in salutation*. It was then common practice for larger vessels of the same nationality in the trade to discharge a five-gun salute when coming alongside one another.

This also explained his sighting of a vessel apparently riding to the *Worcester*'s stern. At a distance of four miles and viewed from a certain angle, any vessel anchoring over the same patch could easily be mistaken for being in tow or moored to the *Worcester*. Indeed, the surgeon was right in only one detail – the meaning of the term 'busking' as referring to the wholly innocent activity of tacking a vessel back against the wind.

The defence went on to maintain that May's description of finding the deck of the *Worcester* heaped with bales and chests on his arrival, was a typical scene when trading off a shallow estuary mouth. In the absence of a deep-water jetty to moor against for loading, goods were delivered alongside in small boats and hoisted on deck. Madder's curse and dismissive comment to the surgeon's enquiry was his crude way of expressing *his concern for the Goods being Dammaged, and [said in] a Tarpallion temper usual in Seamen*. As to the comments he claimed were made by Coge Commodo and the linguister regarding a sea-fight, these were hearsay. Commodo's reference to buying a vessel could easily refer to a purchase made before the event in question.

As for the crewmen's injuries that May suspected as wounds sustained in a battle, these were common occurrences in a working ship. Indeed, it was more than likely that Ferdinando's wound was the result of a 'below deck' squabble that got out of hand. Such an injury he would naturally wish to conceal from his captain, for fear of punishment.

Turning to the other testimonies, the defence dismissed those concerning the conversations that took place while the *Worcester* lay at Burntisland, as hearsay or inference or conjuncture. Haines's ambiguous asides never once made direct reference to the crimes under trial and inferred *no more than that he was using some stratagems to gain his Mistress*. Likewise, the overheard talk of *Wickedness* between the other crewmen could readily apply to any one of the numerous sins to which sailors were susceptible when voyaging abroad and need not be a reference to piracy and murder.

Lastly, the defence turned to the company's seal which Madder once had in his possession and which had been so perfectly described to the jury by the Leith seal-maker. They argued that, as the directors of the Scots Company had taken to signing commissions with other individuals and partnerships in recent years, there were *a hundred ways* that one of their seals might have come into his hands, none of which necessarily involved an act of piracy.

Higgins, for the prosecution, commenced his summing-up with a tirade against the scourge of pirates who were *worse than ravenous Beasts*. After reviewing the evidence given under oath, he concluded by reminding the jury that they had an eye-witness in Ferdinando, who *tho[ugh] a Black, is a legal Witness seeing that, upon full Debate, has been already determined by the Honourable Judges; And indeed besides that, he is not only a Man but a Christian*. So directed, the jury retired on Wednesday 14 March to consider their verdict. They were ordered to return their decision by that Friday.

At ten o'clock on the appointed day, the Chancellor of the Jury, James Fleming of Rathobyres, handed up his note. This was that the jury *by a plurality of votes find, that there is one clear witness to the Piracy, Robbery and Murder libelled, and that there are accumulative and concurring Presumptions, proven for the Piracy and Robbery so libelled; But find that John Reynolds, second mate of the said ship was ashore at the time of the Action libelled.* Reynolds was duly released at the bar.

The news of the guilty verdict on the other fourteen was received in the streets of Edinburgh with undisguised jubilation. Defoe solemnly reported: *I cannot but here take Notice (though with much Concern) that upon the Condemnation of these unhappy Men, there seemed a universal Joy in and about the City; it was the only Discourse for some Days, and every Man thought himself nearly concerned in it; and some could not forbear in Words openly to express their brutal Joy: 'Now', said they, 'we'll Darien 'em: By this they shall see we'll do ourselves Justice.'*

Defoe reckoned that, during their final days of captivity, the prisoners were subjected to a constant barrage of verbal abuse and intimidation, as they

> *were not only insulted with the most opprobrious Language, by such as could get to 'em, but continually worried by the religious Kirk Teachers. The most dismal Threatnings were denounc'd against 'em, and nothing but God's Wrath and eternal Torments in all its Horrors, were to be their Portion, if they died obdurate (as they call'd it) that is, without owning themselves guilty; and all this delivered with that Passion peculiar to that bitter Sett of Men. Nay, so restless were they, that even now, after Condemnation, they singled out some they found more terrified by their Cant, and assur'd 'em of Life if they would ingenuously acknowledge the Crimes they were condemned for; and, at last, worked so far upon Haines and Linsey [Linsteed], that they brought them to own almost what they pleased.*

On 28 March 1705 all this pressure paid off. George Haines not only confessed, but turned belated Queen's Witness to save his neck. From his cell in the Canongate Tolbooth he gave a new sworn declaration in front of Judge Forbes, declaring that *after the ship herein mentioned was seized, he saw the men which were from, killed and murdered with pole axes and cutlases, and saw their dead bodies putt into the sloop & soon after thrown overboard, and to the best of [his] knowledge, the said men were Scots ... having heard them speak the Scots language. And further declared that the ship seized was understood by the crew of the Worcester to have been Captain Drummond's ship ...*

He went on to identify Madder as the leader of the attack and claimed that he had withheld this information for fear that his information would have caused the Scottish *Government [to be] offended, And obliged to deall harshly* with him. Defoe, rather ghoulishly, later elaborated on this confession by having him state that when the crew turned pirate, *every one of 'em was let Blood, which they mixed together, and after every Man had drank part, they all swore to Secrecy.*

Haines's sensational statement was immediately leaked to the *Edinburgh Gazette*. It provided some further embellishments and released an article the following day stating *that the vessel taken on the Malabar Coast was a Ship belong to our* Indian *and* African *Company, Commanded by Capt. Drummond; and that they were murdered all the Men on board her, by chopping off some of their heads with a Hatchet, and tying others Back to Back, and throwing them in the Sea.*

This confession to the gruesome murder of the Scottish crew put the verdict beyond all shadow of a doubt for most patriots. With the first executions scheduled in six days' time, these latest revelations struck the spark to the tinder-dry emotions of the greatly feared Edinburgh mob. Even the right-minded burghers, who had previously balked at this travesty of Scottish Justice, dropped all reservations. Defoe recalled that *as soon as their Confessions were made publick, the Gentry, as well as the Mob, was transported with Rage, and the poor Wretches were blackened and reviled in a shameful Manner; and so violent was the Torrent of their Fury, that it reached even their Council for their Tryals, and they were obliged, for their own Safety, to withdraw into the Country.*

In the absence of any direct intervention by her Scottish Privy Councillors, the Queen's hands were tied. At the insistence of her English Councillors she requested a short reprieve. This was duly approved by her Scottish Councillors sitting in Edinburgh – but they would go no further. To all intents and purposes, this trial had been conducted with due process and diligence. For the monarch to intervene with a pardon for Green and his crew would be to usurp Scottish Justice. Such a move could only be interpreted as riding roughshod over Scottish national sentiment, in an effort to placate, yet again, the interests of the English East India Company.

In England, the dire events unfolding in Edinburgh were viewed with horror, anguish and anger. On the streets of London, hack writers were hard at work churning out tracts that claimed to expose the callous and murderous designs of the Scots. They claimed that the two 'black' witnesses had been hurriedly baptised as Christians for the occasion, kept in strict isolation until the trial and had since been poisoned in their cells. Divine retribution had already struck down the scurrilous surgeon May, as he had dropped dead from an uncontrollable nosebleed at the end of his testimony – certain proof, the newsmongers claimed, that he had borne false witness against Green and his crewmen.

The opportunity was not missed by the Royal Company's lobbyists in the English Parliament who were pushing for further retaliatory legislation. This was in the form of the draconian Aliens Act that would exclude the Scots from owning, working or trading in England, *if a nearer and more compleat Union be not made.*

From daybreak of the first scheduled executions, huge and ugly crowds were lining the way from Edinburgh Castle to Leith Sands, baying for blood and screaming their incessant chant *No Reprieve!* Tens of thousands had poured into Edinburgh, many armed and determined not to be denied their moment of vengeance on the English treachery of the past decade. The fact that two of the men hanged that day, Madder and Simpson, were Scotsmen did not seem to matter.

Only a handful of the Scottish Privy Councillors dared show their faces at Old Parliament House to consider the new evidence from Portsmouth and Queen's latest plea. Most had arrived early in the morning so as to avoid running the gauntlet of the crowds that were massing along the Royal Mile. As Defoe reported: *the Mob perceiving, imagin'd [the Council meeting] 'twas in order to a further Reprieve or Pardon; immediately all Shops were shut up, and the streets filled with incredible Numbers of Men, Women and Children, calling for Justice upon those English Murtherers. The Lord Chancellour Seafield's Coach happening to pass by, they stopp'd it, broke the Sashes, haul'd him out, and oblig'd him to promise Execution should speedily be done before he could get from 'em.*

In such an atmosphere of life-threatening intimidation, this rump of besieged Councillors decided to dismiss the affidavits of the two returned sailors from the *Speedy Return* as *only attested copies* and to proceed with the executions. In doing so, they chose to believe that they were upholding the integrity of Scottish justice in the face of southern interference whilst averting rioting and bloodshed on the streets of Edinburgh.

With their fate confirmed, the three condemned men, Green, Madder and Simpson, were escorted from Edinburgh Castle under heavy military guard. Green was visibly bewildered and still held faith in a last-minute pardon. Madder and Simpson were reported to appear resigned to their fate and remained silent as they took their seats in the cart.

Penny broadsheets purporting to be Greens and Madder's *Last Dying Words* had been selling briskly on the streets days before. Both these testaments maintained their innocence and passionately decried the injustice done to them.

One English gentleman in the crowd reported that as the condemned men trundled past, the jeering crowds *huzza'd in triumph as it were, and insulted [them] with the sharpest and most bitter Invectives.* Captain Robertson, in charge of the guard escorting them to the gibbet, calculated that around eighty thousand people had turned out for this macabre spectacle.

At Leith Sands, with the *Worcester* plainly in sight across the Forth, the City hangman prepared the threesome for their step into eternity. Captain Green twice stopped him from pulling the hood over his head, so that he might look for the rider who would bring the Queen's pardon. After which he seemed to have accepted the inevitable and struggled no more. The ladder was then kicked from under him.

It is significant that, breaking with the Establishment's traditional treatment of pirates, the bodies of the three were not hung in chains but conveyed back to their lodgings. There Mrs Barclay, assisted by the Captain of the Guard, washed and prepared them for a Christian burial, away from the clutches of the mob. During the removal of their coffins, Captain Robertson had to draw his sword to fight back an inflamed rabble intent on abusing the bodies.

In the aftermath of this great tragedy, much soul-searching was undertaken on both sides of the border. The politicians, having witnessed the terrifying power of the baying mob, stepped back from the abyss of further bloodletting. The young Duke of Argyll, as a Queen's Commissioner, arranged for the remaining prisoners to be quietly released and provided them with sufficient monies from his own purse to see them safely back to London.

The *Worcester* was not released. In a final and frantic piece of legal wrangling, the solicitors for the Company of Scotland had the pirate status of this vessel (henceforth the property of the Crown) revoked in favour of that of 'a prize', in reprisal for the seizure of the *Annandale*.

Even this did not save the private possessions of the hanged men being auctioned off as the property of pirates, with Secretary Roderick McKenzie first in line to acquire those of Captain Green. For a few shillings he bought Green's Eastern curios: two ostrich eggs, a tiger skin and an Indian lance and bow, and his Bible.

The principal owner of the *Worcester*, Thomas Bowery, had been the driving force behind the petitions to the Queen for a reprieve. After the executions, he compiled and had published in London *The Case of the Owners and Freighters of the Ship* Worcester, *... and also the Case of the late Capt. Thomas Green ... executed in Scotland for Pretended Piracy and Murder.* In this document he assembled the testimonies of those witnesses who had either been dismissed or unavailable at the time of the trial.

Of the latter group was that of Captain Grandell of the East Indiaman *Aureng-Zeb.* This respected captain claimed that at Quilon, near the port of Anjango, he had exchanged five-gun salutes, over a period of three days, with Green on the *Worcester*. This meeting happened around the time of the alleged attack on the *Speedy Return*. He stated that Green had been driven into Quilon by stress of weather but had been good enough to send over water to him for his sick crewmen. Furthermore, in all his time on the Malabar Coast, he had never heard any mention of an act of piracy at this time.

The other statements included were those taken from the two returned sailors from the *Speedy Return* and the crewmen from the *Worcester* who had escaped over the border before the arrests. All these statements supported Captain Green's denial of any wrongdoing.

The one statement which held new information was that taken from Elizabeth Robison. She was the wife of Andrew, the convicted gunner's mate. She claimed to have new evidence that discredited the *Worcester*'s surgeon, Charles May. She related how she had rushed to Edinburgh from London on hearing of her husband's arrest. On the night before his trial, she sought out the surgeon at his lodgings and confronted him about his testimony, which would condemn her husband to hang for piracy. May was in a flippant mood and claimed that *what he had done would harm no Man*. She then asked him specifically about his key statement – seeing a mysterious ship lying to the stern of the *Worcester*. After much cajoling, he eventually conceded it was a *Country Boat* (native coastal craft) and not another European-built East Indiaman.

Mrs Robison was, by then, quite sure that he had been bribed by someone to maintain the myth that the vessel could have been the missing *Speedy Return*. She pursued him on this matter and he finally told her that, during his enforced stay in

Edinburgh Castle, Lady Mary, the fourteen-year-old daughter of the Governor, Lord Leven, had been his constant companion. This lady had proved highly persuasive and arranged a payment of 150 guineas for his deposition, as it was to be heard in court.

May also told Mrs Robison that Lady Mary had in her possession a letter written by the steward Haines to his father in London. He had given it to George Kitchen to be delivered (presumably after his failed escape bid to Kinghorn), but it been taken from this English crewman before he fled over the border. In his letter, Haines *solemnly Declared the Innocency of Capt. Green and his Crew* to his father.

The exact truth behind the trial, which caused the polarisation of opinion in the two Kingdoms, may never be known. Of the three central witnesses for the prosecution, two (Ferdinando and May) died (of natural causes) in Edinburgh within weeks of the executions. The third, Francisco, took a berth on a visiting Dutch warship and was never heard of again.

As for Captain Green's *Last Dying Words*, the general consensus on both sides of the border was that this was the work of a hack writer close to him in the days before his execution. Indeed, one cynical southern observer claimed that a copy had been sent to one of the London owners of the *Worcester* eight days before the hanging. He identified the author as William Burnet, one of the errand runners for the defence lawyers. Thereafter, this unscrupulous clerk was known as 'Coge Commodo' for his mercenary act. This nickname was, apparently, first bestowed on him by the coal-stealers of Edinburgh.

Opinion as to the fairness of the verdict remained firmly drawn along political lines. The supporters of a Union between Scotland and England held that Green and his crew were innocent men, whilst those against the Union held firm to their belief that they were guilty as charged and deserved to hang.

With modern hindsight, it would seem a remarkable coincidence that Defoe, writing twenty years later about the exploits of Bowen, noted that this pirate once sold an English East Indiaman to native merchants at Callequillon. This transaction took place only months before the arrival of the *Speedy Return* and the *Content* at Madagascar and the *Worcester* off the Malabar Coast. It may well be that this was the vessel to which that Coge Commodo was referred in his conversation with May.

Whatever the real story behind the drama of Captain Green, the trial had the effect of demonstrating the immensity of Scottish disaffection with its overbearing southern neighbour and shocked both establishments into seeking a way round the impasse. That same year, the Queen ordered her Commissioners to assemble in London to set about implementing a full 'incorporating' Union between the two nations, as a final solution to the schism. The first Article was the surrender of Scotland's national sovereignty to create 'one kingdom' in exchange for Scotland's full admission into the (new) British overseas empire.

While they set about this delicate and highly contentious business, the Company of Scotland tried to reassert its authority and revive its fortunes with yet another passage to the East. In December 1706, five months after the proposed Articles of the Union had been presented to the Queen, they signed an agreement with a group of Edinburgh merchants – James Gordon, James Majoribanks and Robert Forrester (all jury members at the trial). This was for a last-gasp voyage to China via Madagascar under the Company Patent.

This venture employed the *Neptune* galley (200 tons), under the command of the Edinburgh merchant and master, James Miller. She was particularly well armed against the threat of pirates and against the agents of the English Companies with twenty-four 'great guns' and fifty men.

She sailed from Leith in January 1707, just four months before the Union and the dissolution of the Scots Company, carrying the usual mixed cargo of strong liquor and small arms. This venture ended in the same way as that of the *Speedy Return* and the *Concord*. The *Neptune* was taken by the Madagascan pirate John Halsey.

The visit of the *Neptune* to Madagascar did, however, significantly contribute to the demise of this great pirate nest. As the pirate hunter Captain Alexander Hamilton commented, *the Scots ship commanded by one Millar did the public more service in destroying them, than all the chargeable squadrons that have been sent in quest of them; for, with a cargo of strong ale and brandy, which he carried to sell them ... he killed above 500 of them by carousing, although they took his ship and cargo as a present from him, and his men entered, most of them into the society of the pirates.* The 'chargeable squadron' he was referring to was that of HMS *Scarborough* and HMS *Severn* under Commodore Littlejohn, which had cruised around Madagascar between 1703 and 1705 to no great effect.

This unintentional massacre of pirates by alcohol abuse heralded a period of respite from the scourge of the Black Flag in the Indian Ocean. To capitalise on this cull, a committee was set up by the Board of Trade in 1707. On this board sat the owner of the *Worcester*, Thomas Bowery. It recommended offering a new pardon to the survivors of Miller's visit, which was duly granted by the newly constituted (British) Privy Council.

This uneasy peace in the Indian Ocean lasted twelve years. It was finally broken when the New Providence pirates Edward England, John Taylor and Olivier La Bouche, arrived in Madagascan waters from West Africa in 1719, in good time to intercept Captain James Macrae on the *Cassandra*.

The Last Pirates in Scottish Waters, 1821

CHAPTER 11

Heaman & Gautier:
the Last Pirates in
Scottish Waters

Just after eight o'clock on the morning of 9 January 1822, three carriages left Edinburgh City Council Chambers. They made their way down the Royal Mile and across the North Bridge to the Bridewell, the city's main jail, at the foot of Calton Hill.

In the first carriage were the Lord Provost and his main officials, resplendent in their civic robes and white gloves. They were holding their ceremonial halberds (long-handled 'hook-and-bill' axes) which denoted their status as Sergeants-at-Arms, the defenders of the city. The second carriage conveyed lesser officials and Father Wallace, a Roman Catholic priest. The third carriage was reserved for the presiding minister, the Reverend Campbell, and James Porteous, the chaplain to the jail.

The great gates of the prison were already open in anticipation of their arrival. In the courtyard was a small black open cart with the two condemned pirates: the 36-year-old Swede Peter Heaman of Karlskrona, and the 24-year-old Frenchman François Gautier of Le Havre. They were manacled and seated with their backs to the driver. Surrounding the cart on which this pathetic pair sat, dressed as they were in their crumpled and faded brown jackets and sailor's white trousers, was a phalanx of police on foot. The mounted troops of the 3rd Dragoons flanked each side.

Crowds had gathered on the high open ground of Calton Hill that overlooked the jail. From there they had a grandstand view of the departure of the solemn procession which took the two men the mile and a quarter to Leith Sands and the gallows. As they turned the corner at Waterloo Place on to the top of Leith Walk, Heaman became aware of the jeering crowds lining the pavements. Most were women and children, so he felt compelled to stand up and make little nervous bows to them as he trundled past. Gautier, according to the observing reporter of the *Edinburgh Evening Courant*, sat in a daze throughout, utterly consumed by his own thoughts.

At the bottom of the Walk, the Vice-Admiral of Scotland and dignitaries from the port of Leith were waiting to join the procession on its final leg down Constitution Street and on to the Naval Yard. On the open sands, fifty yards out from the north-western corner of this yard, was the gibbet on a raised platform. Awaiting his charges was Thomas Williams, the much-employed city executioner. The *Courant's* reporter reckoned that, by then, in excess of forty thousand onlookers had gathered for the grim spectacle.

As Williams went about his business preparing his clients, the Reverend Campbell led the singing of the 51st Psalm. The reporter remarked that the two condemned men appeared to join in. Campbell then read out a solemn statement from the Swede admitting his guilt, thanking those responsible for his fair trial and warning all those assembled of the dangers of straying from the path of righteous living. After prayers, the Frenchman spoke only to ask for God's mercy and, after briefly shaking hands with his old sailing partner, *drop't the signal* to the hangman. The trapdoor, a recent innovation introduced by the notorious Deacon Brodie, fell open beneath them and the great bell of the South Leith Church struck the first chime of a slow and solitary toll.

After they had been pronounced dead, their bodies were cut down. To deter the scavengers in the mob, the dragoons were detailed to accompany the corpses back up to the Old Town and Dr Munro's anatomy classroom at the University for dissection *as pursuant to their sentence*.

The members of Edinburgh's Establishment who had attended were greatly relieved. With such a tumultuous gathering, things could have so easily got out of hand, *but owing to the excellent manner in which everything was arranged, not the slighted accident happened*. There was also all-round satisfaction with the way the culprits had gone to their death decent, resigned and penitent under the firm guidance of the ministers and the priest.

Heaman and Gautier had been found guilty and hanged for *piratically seizing the brig* Jane *of Gibraltar on her voyage from Gibraltar to Brazil, freighted with 38,180 Spanish dollars ... [in doing so] murdering Thomas Johnson, the master and James Paterson, a seaman* on the night of 6 June 1821.

The *Jane* was a small 'Aphrodite' brig of around 100 tons burthen. She was owned by a Jewish merchant, Moses Levy of Gibraltar. Her master was the well-respected Thomas Johnson, who had brought with him to his new command Andrew Camelier, a 17-year-old Maltese cabin boy and star witness at the trial in Edinburgh.

The other six crewmen were all new signings who had recently been paid off at Gibraltar from the *Araquebassa*. Peter Heaman was appointed mate and François Gautier the cook. Of the four deck hands, three were Scots: James Paterson, Robert Strachan and Peter Smith (the last two lads from Montrose). The remaining crewman was a Portuguese sailor, Joanna Dhura, sailing under the name 'John Hard'. Apart from Captain Johnson, only Heaman had any knowledge of the higher art of navigation.

Two days after 'smoking' (fumigating) the *Jane*, the cargo manifest was completed with the stowing of eight barrels containing tens of thousands of Spanish 'hard' silver coins. These were destined for Portuguese merchants in Bahia and St Salvador in Brazil. The rest of the cargo was made up of the natural bounty of Iberia: thirty pipes of sweet oil; ninety-eight barrels of beeswax; fifteen bags of aniseed; along with thirty-four bundles of duty-stamped paper. Only the master and the mate knew the contents of the eight barrels delivered on board on the last afternoon before sailing. Hanging in the captain's tiny cabin space were seven muskets and one pistol. These were the captain's only defence against pirate attack or insurrection by the crew.

The *Jane* cleared out of Gibraltar on 18 May. By the evening of 6 June she was in mid-Atlantic, five sailing days west of the Canaries and making good progress in fine weather and a light wind. At eight o'clock the three-man watch changed. On this occasion the captain took his turn on the relief watch with Strachan and Dhura. At midnight this watch duly changed, with the new watch-leader Heaman accompanied by Paterson and Gautier (who was replacing Smith, who was confined to his hammock with a badly-gashed foot). This was the opportunity for which the mate and the cook had been waiting.

Captain Johnson retired to his diminutive stern berth and fell asleep. He remained fully dressed, for he had received a series of warnings from Strachan that the crew knew about the special cargo and that a plot was afoot to take the vessel.

What happened next varies greatly between two versions: one given by the ordinary seamen held together in a cell of Edinburgh's Old Tolbooth; and that of the mate and the cook held in a separate cell. Both groups had adequate time to perfect their story as they were incarcerated for four months before the trial.

The only witness to the double murder was Camelier, the cabin boy. Around two o'clock in the morning he was asleep in his bunk close to the captain's when he was suddenly awakened by a shot fired at very close range. In his fright he instantly scrambled up on deck. There he witnessed Heaman repeatedly bludgeoning Paterson with the butt of a musket as the stricken Scot cried: *Murder, murder, God Almighty save my soul, for I am murdered now!*

As Paterson's lifeless body rolled under the stowed ship's boat, Captain Johnson staggered up from his cabin crying *What is this? What is this?* Blood was streaming from the right side of his head. The cook sprang on the captain and knocked him to the deck with his musket butt, and the mate joined in, raining blows on the prostrate master. Heaman then rushed to the forecastle hatch and cried down, *All hands on deck to shorten sail!*

At this point the testimonies of the other three crewmen make their contribution to the chain of events that followed. Dhura appeared first from the fore-hatch and was allowed past, but Strachan was threatened by Heaman with an axe and driven back down to rejoin Smith below. The hatch was then slammed shut on them. On deck and in fear of their lives, Dhura and Camelier were forced to help the cook dispose of the two bodies overboard. Paterson's body was weighed down with an iron piece of an old anchor whilst some stones from the ballast were tied to the legs of the captain. As the captain was pushed over, he let out a moan before disappearing into the dark sea. The terrified cabin boy, now reduced to tears, pleaded with Heaman for his life. After a moment's silence Heaman told him to go forward and stay there.

The seizure of the *Jane* had taken the two new pirates less than six minutes. To ensure their control and ability to sail the brig the two other crewmen had to be mastered. To achieve this, the mate nailed down the fore-hatch and had a tarpaulin tightly fitted over it. The cabin boy was told to mix up some flour and water. The mate used this paste to seal round the tarpaulin edges. The mate then went below and bored two holes through the bulkhead into the forecastle. He then lit a smoke bomb made from tar and barrel staves and shoved it hard against the holes.

For two nights and a day the entombed Strachan and Smith endured this ordeal in total darkness. On the second day they were brought up and tied to the studsail boom on the deck and were offered some food, water and money if they would take the brig's small oared boat and leave. This they refused to do as they were in the middle of the ocean; and so they were forced under hatches again.

On the third morning, Dhura begged Heaman to let them up before they died. As the two groped their way up the two armed pirates were waiting for them. Gautier simply said: *You go in the sea!* The two sailors begged for their lives and said they would turn pirate if spared. Heaman made them swear on and then kiss a Bible that the cook held out. They swore never to tell what had happened on the *Jane* and agreed to assist in the navigation of the brig from here on. That concluded, they were set to cleaning the blood-splattered decks.

The cabin boy was assigned the revolting task of cleaning out the captain's bunk. From his description of what he saw, it is plain that Gautier had discharged his pistol point blank against the sleeping master's head, using a pillow to avoid a flash burn. He went on to relate that the cook was later much amused to pick up from the deck the flattened musket ball that had fallen out of the captain's head wound when he had finally been rolled over the side.

The forced sailors all testified that Captain Johnson had been a quiet and good-tempered master who had done nothing to incite or deserve such a death. Indeed, he had even taken the time to treat the cook's bound-up arm with camphor when he first came aboard at Gibraltar.

Heaman's plan was to land the hoard of silver coins on a remote beach – somewhere in France, Ireland or Scotland. The *Jane* would be then be scuttled. The brig was subsequently set on a course due north. For the next four weeks the crew were made to sleep on deck under an awning, with one of the pirates always on watch. During the day, the crew were put to making bags out of some old thin canvas into which the silver coins were decanted from the barrels with a tin pint mug. These were then concealed behind the bulkheads and between the vessel's side and panels. The incriminating marked barrels were destroyed. Heaman and Gautier also took care to burn the brig's manifest, registration and logbook. The captain's personal papers were thrown overboard, tied to muskets which were surplus to the mate's and the cook's requirements.

To implicate the forced men and buy their co-operation, the pirates promised them a share in the loot once they were all safely ashore. The crew were then rehearsed in their new guise as the crew of the American brig *Rover*, bound for Archangel from New York. This ruse was used successfully during one close encounter with another vessel during their passage north. As they approached Ireland the weather turned cold and the crew were allowed to sleep below decks.

Landfall was made off Sligo, Northern Ireland on 18 July. Three days later the *Jane* put into Vatersay Bay opposite the island of Barra in the Outer Hebrides. There the mate, dressed in the dead captain's green coat, rowed ashore with a considerable amount of sweet oil and beeswax broached from the cargo. Calling himself 'Captain Rogers of New York' he quickly engaged a local young merchant, Neil McNeil, with a deal to exchange his wares for a large open fishing boat that could step a sail. This deal was struck over dinner at McNeil's father's house, after which the mate returned. His purchase was delivered the same day and hoisted onto the deck of the *Jane*. The pirates now had the means to effect their plan to get ashore with the loot unnoticed.

The mate had gleaned from his hosts over dinner that an armed Revenue cutter was cruising the area through which he intended to return to the Vatersay anchorage that very night. So forewarned, Heaman immediately ordered the *Jane* northwards. The crew was informed that if stopped by the cutter, their story was that pirates had boarded and killed the captain and the helmsman. Indeed, at the first sight of the cutter they were commanded to throw their best clothes overboard so as to make it look as if they had been robbed and left destitute.

Heaman's new plan was to round Cape Wrath and scuttle the *Jane* off 'Johnny Groat's' House. Sailing past the town of Stornoway on the Isle of Lewis, however, he decided not to risk being boarded and to execute his plan a day early. Off Tolsta

Head, some ten miles up the coast, he ordered the fishing boat lowered and brought alongside. As the money sacks were being loaded, Smith, Dhura and the cabin boy were sent below with tools to drill holes and stove in the planking of the hull to scuttle the *Jane*. This they did with the greatest trepidation, fearing that Heaman would shut the hatches on them and leave them to go down with the brig.

By nine of the evening, as the daylight started to fade, the *Jane* was settling low in the sea. The water pouring in had already risen above the level of the cabin floor. All six crewmen hastened onto the fishing boat, already overloaded with the sheer weight of the money sacks and their sea chests. As they tried to cast off, the unattended brig began to go about on her own, threatening to run down the wallowing fishing boat before they could get under way.

To save the situation, Heaman leapt back on board the brig and reset her top square sail to stand her off on the opposite reach before scrambling back to the fishing boat. As the *Jane* made off for the rocky headland and her wrecking, they stepped the sail on the fishing boat and finally got under way.

Their intention was to cross the treacherous North Minch that separates the Outer Hebrides from the mainland of Scotland. This passage – twenty-odd miles as the crow flies – is one of the most dangerous in British waters, being highly exposed to the erratic weather patterns of the North Atlantic. They were not long set on their chosen course when the sea got up and the waves began to broach over the sides of the overloaded boat. Unable to go on without courting disaster, they turned back towards Lewis.

During that night the rising wind and fierce tide swept the boat twelve miles back down the coast from Tolsta Head, past

Broad Bay and round Chicken Head. It was with some difficulty that they worked the boat behind this headland and into the comparative shelter of the open bay at Swordale.

It was past noon when they attempted to beach the boat. In the high running surf the fishing boat overset on the large stones that made up most of this shoreline. This ended all immediate prospect of putting back out to sea.

Using the overturned boat and sail as a shelter they set up camp on the open beach. Heaman and Gautier were now desperate men, as their discovery would only be a matter of time. The town of Stornoway was only a few miles away and there were farms in the immediate vicinity. In broad daylight, they frantically started to bury the money-bags in various holes along the beach. A few were kept back and hidden in the floor of each of the sea chests. Their intention was probably to return at some future date to retrieve the main body of the loot.

First on the scene was the 60-year-old local farmer, John Murray, who was soon joined by his inquisitive neighbours. Their news of strangers on the beach quickly got back to the agents of government in Stornoway. Late that night four armed boatmen of the Customs Service turned up to make enquiries. They first suspected that they were smugglers from a lugger which had been seen skulking offshore.

Close behind them arrived their superior, the Surveyor of Customs, Roderick McIver, accompanied by his son. Heaman was ready for them with his latest story. This was that he was 'George Sadwell', the mate of the *Betsy* of New York. He claimed that this brig, owned by his father, had been lost off Barra Head days before. He had since quarrelled with his stranded captain as to what to do next and had gone off with one of the long-boats with these five crewmen to get help.

He might have got away with it had not the customs officers rummaged in the sea chests and found the bags of Spanish silver dollars. McIver, unaware of the fortune buried under the rocks of the beach, was highly suspicious and decided to go back to Stornoway and check his shipwreck story. He later recalled that as he tried to take down notes *it rained so fast that the names were obliterated as soon as written*. He left two of his boatmen in charge of the suspects.

He had only gone a hundred yards from the beach when he was waylaid by the cabin boy who blurted out his story of piracy and murder in his broken English. McIver quickly led him away and out of sight of the encampment. They only stopped when they were safely on top of the cliff that overlooked the beach. There McIver heard the whole gruesome story while he watched Gautier and Heaman frantically search for the lad below.

His first act was to send back his other two boatmen with the explicit order that they were to keep all *the country people* (the local spectators) close to hand in case the pirates tried to escape or attempted to enlist their help to relaunch their boat. If so, they were instructed to stave in its sides. Reaching the hamlet of Swordale he arranged for some local men to reinforce those standing guard on the beach.

By midnight he was back in Stornoway where the cabin boy spilled out the location of the concealed silver hoard – in the folds of hammocks and buried in holes on the shore. McIver finally grasped just how desperate these men were and what they had to lose. His first action was to send his son straight back with a large armed posse to secure all those at the encampment as prisoners.

At first light McIver returned with his clerk and the laborious business of recovering and recording the hidden caches got under way. All in all, just over 31,000 coins were recovered, leaving 7,000 unaccounted for against the insurer's copy of the cargo manifest.

Heaman and Gautier had, understandably, a different story to tell – this time, of an irate Captain Johnson who had shot Paterson in a fit of rage over his incompetence at the helm which had cost him a spar. In the struggle that ensued to overpower the master, Gautier's arm was broken and Johnson accidentally killed. They blamed the other crew members for the decision to steal the coins and the Montrose men in particular for the choice of landing in Scotland. The Prosecutor for the High Court of Admiralty, Alexander Kydd, rejected their version and moved on to that of the ordinary seamen. So acquitted, they then became the main witnesses for the prosecution.

On 26 November 1821, the trial of the mate and cook for the crimes of *Piracy & Murder* began at the Tolbooth. From the outset there was a language barrier to be overcome. Gautier claimed to speak only French fluently, the witness Dhura only Portuguese and the main witness from Stornoway, John Murray, only Gaelic – *not fully understanding English*. Interpreters were found in Edinburgh, after which the case proceeded quickly.

The fifteen-man jury found against the accused. A condemned man, Gautier wrote home to his Spanish wife that he was *ill and in hospital*, while it was rumoured that Heaman's only verbal request was that his mother never be told of his crime and tragic end.

This was to be the last trial and hanging of pirates in Scotland. After 1830 the High Court of Admiralty of Scotland ceased to exist. Common Law proceedings relating to incidents in Scottish waters now came under the jurisdiction of the Scottish High Court of Judiciary. All matters relating to International Maritime Law were, henceforth, deemed the exclusive business of the High Court of Admiralty of Great Britain sitting in London.

CHAPTER 12

Conclusion

The 'Golden Age of Piracy' effectively came to an end in April 1722, when the last members of the New Providence 'House of Lords' were strung up at Cape Coast Castle. Without this core of ruthless pirates, the cycle of seizing vessels and forcing men to maintain their large pirate companies was broken.

In any case, by then the game was all but up. Their rampage across the Caribbean, African and Indian seas over the past four years had finally spurred the governments into taking unequivocal and direct action. The old policy of 'carrot and stick' was abandoned – there would be no more pardons, only relentless pursuit by naval squadrons. Likewise, the old accommodation struck up between a retiring pirate and a colonial governor became a thing of the past. Corrupt officials were weeded out and replaced by more resolute men who could not be so easily bribed.

Those pirates that were not caught and hanged – such as Edward England and John Taylor – got out of 'the business' and found sanctuary where they could: in their case, one under the protection of old mates on Madagascar and the other in the coastguard service of the Spanish. For the few remaining pirate companies that still pursued their chosen profession, it was only a matter if time before they were captured and killed. The rapid rise of royal navies and the armed fleets of the great trading companies gave the offensive power needed to enforce the Law of Nations in every corner of the planet. In the Caribbean the South Seas Company fitted out pirate chasers that assisted the navy to clear out the last of them. The East India Company performed the same service in the Red Sea and the Indian Ocean.

Prizes were also becoming tough nuts to crack for a single pirate company, as the fledging marine insurance industry took to rewarding merchant captains who fought off pirates.

For the Scots merchants, their losses to Black Flag pirates and Barbary corsairs had a profound impact on their business schemes. With full legal access to the Americas after the Act of Union (1707), they gave up, for the time being, their attempts to enter the East Indies and the African slave trades in favour of shipping tobacco and sugar. These trades kept their vessels plying the North Atlantic routes and away from the southern oceans where sporadic acts of piracy continued to happen after 1722.

The incentive to turn pirate in North Atlantic waters had, by then, virtually disappeared, as demonstrated by the paltry haul of personal valuables looted by the Orcadian pirate, John Gow, during his winter cruise off the Iberian Peninsula (1724–5). Even where the lure was irresistible – such as the barrels of silver dollars which tempted the opportunists Heaman and Gautier – the chances of getting clean away by landing on a remote Scottish shore were slight. By the time of their capture in 1821, the agents of government were firmly entrenched in every port in Scotland and Revenue cruisers patrolled the coastline. The trial of Heaman and Gautier marks the end of Scotland's sporadically rich contribution to Pirate History, the legacy of which has since reached the attention of the world through the pens of Defoe, Scott and Robert Louis Stevenson.

Select Bibliography

Manuscripts
India Office Records, Home Miscellaneous (British Library) (*H series*) Online
    searchable catalogue

National Archives of Scotland

    High Court of Admiralty of Scotland
    AC9/ 722 & 742 & 762 & 770 (Craignish pirates)
    AC9/718 & 762 (*Loyalty* slaver)
    AC9/1042 (*Hannover* slaver)
    AC9/126 & 150 & 162 (Captain Green)

    Crown Office
    AD/ 14/21 (Heaman & Gautier pirates)
    Gifts & Deposits (*GD series*) Online searchable catalogue

Primary Printed

NEWSPAPERS

Aberdeen Journal
Edinburgh Evening Courant
Edinburgh Gazette
Glasgow Mercury
London Gazette

PAMPHLETS

Anon, *Observations Made in England, on the trial of Captain Green and the speech at his Death* (London & Edinburgh, 1705)

——, *The tryal of Captain Green and his crew . . . for Piracy. Robbery & Murder* (Edinburgh, 1705)

——, *The murther of Capt. Green* (London, 1705)

——, *Some Cursory Remarks on a Late Printed Paper called The last Speeches and Dying Words of Captain Thomas Green* (Edinburgh, 1705)

Booth, B. A. & E. Mehew (eds)., *The letters of Robert Louis Stevenson* (London, 1994–1995)

Calendar of State Papers (54 series)

Hamilton, A., *A new account of the East Indies* (Edinburgh, 1727)

——, *An answer to an anonymous libel, entitled, Articles exhibited against Lord Archibald Hamilton* (London, 1718)

Herries, W. (attrib.), *A defence of the Scots abdicating Darien* (Edinburgh, 1700)

Luntly, R., *The Last speech and dying words of Richard Luntly . . . for crimes of piracy and robbery* (Edinburgh, 1721)

Mitchell, J. (attrib), *A full account of the proceedings in relation to Capt. Kidd – in two letters* (London, 1701)

Mowat, S. & Graham, E.J. (eds), The High Court of Admiralty Records (1627–1750) [CD-ROM] (Dunfermline, 2005)

Proclamation(s) for the more effectual reducing and suppressing piracy (London, 1688 & 1696 & 1719& 1721 & 1729)

Snelgrave, W., *A New Account of Some Parts of Guinea, And the Slave-Trade* (London, 1734)

Stuart, A., *Report on the trial of Peter Heaman and Francois Gautiez or Gautier, for the crimes of Piracy and Murder* (Edinburgh, 1821)

SECONDARY PRINTED

Arnot, H., *Collection and abridgement of celebrated criminal trials in Scotland, from A.D. 1536-1784* (Edinburgh, 1785)

Behrendt, S.D. & Graham, E.J. 'African Merchants, Notables and the Slave Trade at Old Calabar, 1720: Evidence from the National Archives of Scotland', *History in Africa*, vol. 30 (2003)

Bialuschewski, A. 'Between Newfoundland and the Malacca Straits: a survey of the Golden Age of Piracy, 1695–1725, *Mariner's Mirror*, vol. 90 (May 2204)

Botting, D. (ed.), *The Pirates* (Amsterdam, 1979)

Course, A.G., *Pirates of the Eastern Seas* (London, 1966)

Defoe, D., (attrib), *A General History of the robberies and murders of the most notorious Pyrates by Captain Charles Johnson* (London, 1724) & subsequent editions notable 1726 vols, I & II

——, *A History of the Union of Great Britain* (Edinburgh, 1709)

——, *An account of the conduct and proceedings of the late John Gow, alias Smith, Captain of the late pirates . . . on board the* George gally (London, 1725)

Downing, C., *A compendium history of the Indian Wars . . . and forces of Angria the Pyrate* (undated)

Gosse, P.H.G., *The Pirates Who's Who* (London, 1924)

——, *The history of piracy* (London, 1932)

Graham. E.J., *A Maritime History of Scotland 1650–1790* (East Linton, 2002)

Grey, C., *Pirates of the Eastern Seas (1618–1723)* (London, 1933)

Innes, B., *A Book of Pirates* (London, 1966)

Insh, G.P., *Darien Shipping Papers* (Edinburgh, 1924)

Prebble, J., *The Darien Disaster* ((London, 2002)

Pyle, H., *Howard Pyle's Book of Pirates* (London, 1921)

Scott, Sir W., *The Pirate* (London, 1908)

Stevenson, R.L., *Treasure Island* (London, 1933)

Talboys Wheeler, J., *Annals of James Macrae, esq.. Governor of Madras* (Madras, 1862)

Taylor, J., *A Journey to Edenborough in Scotland* (Edinburgh, 1903)

Temple, Sir R. C., *New light on the mysterious tragedy of the 'Worcester'* (London, 1930)

Terry, R.C. (ed.), *R. L. Stevenson: interviews and recollections* (London, 1996)

Watson, G., *John Gow – The Orkney Pirate* (Inverness, 1978)

Index